Competitiveness and Regulation

Government and Competitiveness Project
Seminar Series
Montreal, Quebec
April 1992

Canadian Cataloguing in Publication Data

Main entry under title:

Competitiveness and regulation : government and
   competitiveness project seminar series, Montreal, Quebec,
   April 1992

(Seminar series)
Includes bibliographical references.
ISBN 0-88911-646-6

1. Industry and state - Canada - Congresses. 2. Trade
regulation - Canada - Congresses. I. Hirshhorn, Ronald.
II. Gautrin, Jean-François. III. Queen's University
(Kingston, Ont.). School of Policy Studies. IV. Series:
Seminar series (Kinston, Ont.).

HD3616.C23C6 1993   338.971   C93-094312-0

Contents

Foreword

Governments do much to affect our daily lives. They tax. They spend. They regulate. They redistribute income. As pervasive and vital institutions in Canadian society, it is important that governments be efficient and accountable. If Canada is to be competitive in international markets, it is essential.

Governments touch the lives of us all in many ways and on a daily basis. They set the legal frameworks by which we are governed; they regulate the services we consume; and they directly provide a vast array of goods and services.

Despite this pervasive influence, few of us really appreciate the full range of what governments do. Fewer still understand how those activities affect the performance of the economy. To help address this situation, the prime minister in 1991 requested the Economic Council of Canada to undertake a major project "on the structure of government in Canada and to contribute importantly to the public debate on how governments can achieve their objectives while effectively controlling costs to the private sector."

The Economic Council of Canada ceased operating in June 1992 but the important work of this Project has continued under the auspices of the School of Policy Studies, Queen's University. The Project will generate publications, a series of seminars, and towards the end of 1993, a final report.

The research program of the Project focuses on six dimensions of government: efficient size and jurisdiction, regulation, efficient program delivery, efficient pricing, efficient purchasing and policy-making processes. Bryne Purchase is director of the Project, and is assisted by an Advisory Committee composed of representatives of federal, provincial and municipal governments, and leaders from business, labour and the universities.

This publication reports on a seminar on government regulation organized by Jean-François Gautrin in Montreal in April 1992. The purpose of the seminar was to explore the efficient use of regulation as an instrument of government policy. This publication includes an overview of the seminar, summaries of the papers that were presented and the comments of discussants. A list of participants is appended.

The overview by Ron Hirshhorn and Jean-François Gautrin looks at the role and the limitations of regulation as one of a number of instruments of government policy. There are situations where markets do not work very well, and regulation may be the most appropriate form of intervention. It is necessary, however, to weigh the costs of imperfect markets against the costs of an imperfect regulatory regime. Regulatory systems fail for a number of reasons: those who influence regulatory policy have their own objectives which are not completely consistent with the requirements for economic efficiency; governments lack complete information on the impact of regulation and are unable to fully assess costs and benefits; and there are problems in coordinating the regulatory activities of the different departments and the different levels of government with overlapping or closely related responsibilities.

The overview proceeds from a discussion of these problems to a consideration of the options for regulatory reform. Deregulation is an attractive option where there is no longer a valid rationale for intervention, or where public policy objectives can be addressed by an alternative, less restrictive and less costly form of intervention. An alternative is regulatory reform. This can involve attempts to improve the design, administration, or enforcement of regulations. A major focus in the seminar was on the prospects for improving regulation through the use of market-based incentives in place of existing command-and-control mechanisms.

At the more general level, the overview asks whether the reform of regulation-making processes within government can contribute to better regulation. Major procedural reforms were introduced by the federal government in 1986, but the results are, in some ways, disappointing. Nonetheless, the authors put forward a number of constructive proposals to promote greater transparency and more rigorous analysis of both existing and proposed regulations. They argue that an informed public provides the best prospect for balanced and responsible regulation making.

Judith Maxwell
Associate Director
School of Policy Studies

Competitiveness and Regulation

About the Editors ...

Ronald Hirshhorn is an economic and public policy consultant in Ottawa. He was recently a senior economist with the Royal Commission on National Passenger Transportation. For a number of years, Mr. Hirshhorn was on the senior staff of the Economic Council of Canada. He directed the Council study entitled *Minding the Public's Business*, and has contributed a number of studies in the areas of industrial organization and public policy. He is currently serving as a consultant to the Government and Competitiveness Project.

Jean-François Gautrin is currently working as the coordinator of a World Bank project in Thailand. At the time of this conference, he was a Research Fellow with the Government and Competitiveness Project. He was previously Vice-President in charge of economic studies and special advisor at Lavalin-Econosult. Mr. Gautrin has written widely on public policy issues and managed numerous projects in Canada and abroad.

Towards Efficient Regulation

An Overview by *Ronald Hirshhorn* and
Jean-François Gautrin

Introduction

The study of government regulation has become an industry in its own right. It has attracted the interest of academics in a number of disciplines (economics, political science, public policy, business), and given rise to a large and growing literature. The Government and Competitiveness Project convened a seminar in Montreal in April 1992 to review selected aspects of this literature and to consider the contribution they can make to the Project's broader inquiry into the impact of government on competitiveness.

As with other seminars conducted by the Government and Competitiveness (G&C) Project, a central underlying focus was on how government affects the allocation of resources. How does government affect the answers society reaches to the basic questions about what to produce, how to produce, and for whom? In the Montreal seminar, these general issues were examined in the context of a particular form of government intervention. A regulation is any rule having the force of law[1] that constrains the behaviour of economic agents; firms and individuals subject to regulation are limited in some way in what they can and cannot do.

Regulation is one way governments attempt to influence the behaviour of individuals and firms. Governments also exercise power through a variety of non-regulatory mechanisms, including exhortation, information disclosure, subsidization, taxation, and public ownership. In other G&C seminars the economic and political characteristics of some of these non-regulatory instruments have received attention. Regulation involves a greater degree of coercion than most other instruments. Rules are established and there is an explicit threat of punishment for non-compliance. Regulation also differs from tax and expenditure instruments because most costs are non-budgetary. Indeed, government regulatory expenditures are like the tip of an iceberg; hidden beneath the surface loom the major regulatory costs borne by private firms.

Have Canadians been made better off by the use of administrative decisions in place of the decisions of individual producers and consumers responding to market incentives? This question can only be addressed through an examination of specific regulations or regulatory programs, and in each case the conclusion will depend on the answer to three subsidiary questions: first, is there a valid rationale for government intervention? Second, has the appropriate form of intervention been selected? Would, for example, the use of an alternative instrument that does not involve legal sanctions, such as subsidies, tax incentives, or information dissemination, have been more appropriate? And third, has the regulatory program been designed and implemented so as to realize the full benefits from the use of this instrument? Although these three questions did not receive uniform coverage at the seminar, they were very much at the heart of the issues being discussed.

Size and Scope

Regulation is pervasive in Canada. Most of our activities as consumers and workers are influenced in some way by regulation. Table 1, which is taken from the Economic Council of Canada (1979), is a useful illustration of the range of activities regulated by the three levels of government. Some of the industries identified in the table, such as electric utilities, telephone, and intercity busing are subject to what is variously referred to as "direct" or "economic" regulation. Here, the focus is on controlling the behaviour of a particular firm, or a group of firms within a particular industry. The government or an independent agency regulates the terms and conditions of production, with this often extending to entry, exit, price and/or rate of return, and type of service. The other major form of regulation is "social regulation." This refers to a diverse set of standards and prohibitions aimed at protecting the environment, reducing health and safety risks for workers and consumers, and promoting fairness in the marketplace and workplace.

Enabling legislation may delegate the power to make regulations to government officials, to agencies or boards, or to occupational and professional bodies. While the activities of "self-regulating" bodies are often overlooked in regulatory discussions, occupational regulation is the focus of a large amount of provincial legislation and it constitutes an important form of government regulation.

Efforts to assess the overall size and importance of regulation in Canada is complicated by the largely hidden nature of regulatory costs. A comprehensive measure would relate to the overall stock of federal, provincial and municipal regulations. The aggregation procedure used in the measure would take account of the varying importance of different regulations as indicated by private and public sector expenditures and other estimated costs (including the "dead-weight losses" attributable to each regulation). At the federal level, we have a partial indication of the importance of regulation at one point in time from the 1985 Ministerial Task Force on Program Review (Nielson Task Force). The Task Force identified 146 federal regulatory programs. These were estimated to involve 34,500 public officials and to cost the government $2.7 billion. Private sector costs associated with these programs were estimated to be at least $30 billion annually. More recent estimates suggest that currently there are in the range of 50,000 public officials involved in the development, administration and enforcement of federal regulations.[2]

Table 1

The Scope of Regulation in Canada

Communications

Broadcasting
    Radio (AM, FM)
    Television
Telecommunications
    Telephone
    Telegraph
    Satellite
    Cable TV

Consumer Protection/ Information

Disclosure (product content labelling, terms of sale, etc.)
False and Misleading Advertising
Sales Techniques (merchandising)
Packaging and Labelling
Prohibited Transactions, e.g., pyramid sales, referral sales
Weights and Measures

Cultural/Recreational

Residency requirements
Language (bilingualism)
Canadian content in broadcasting
Horse Racing
Gambling (lotteries)
Sports
Film, Theatre, Literature, Music, e.g., Canadian content

Energy

Nuclear
Natural Gas
Petroleum
Hydro-electric
Coal

Environmental Management

(a) Pollution Control
    air
    water
    solid waste disposal
(b) Resource Development
    minerals
    forestry
    water
(c) Wildlife Protection
    hunting
    fishing
    parks/reserves
    endangered species

(d) Land Use
    planning/zoning
    development approval
    sub-division
    strata-title
(e) Weather Modification

Financial Markets and Institutions

Banks
Non-banks
    Trust Companies
    Management Companies
    Finance Companies
    Credit Unions/Caisses
    Populaires
Pension Plans
Securities/Commodities Transactions
Insurance

Food Production and Distribution

(a) Agricultural Products Marketing
    pricing
    grading
    storage
    distribution
    entry
    supply
(b) Fisheries (marine, freshwater)
    price
    entry
    quotas
    gear

Framework

Competition Policy
Anti-dumping laws
Foreign Investment Review Act
Bankruptcy laws
Corporation laws
Intellectual and Industrial Property
    Property
    copyright
    industrial design
    patents
    trade marks
Election laws
    contributors
    spending
    reporting

Health and Safety

(a) Occupational Health and Safety

(b) Products – Use
    explosives
    firearms
    chemicals
(c) Product – Characteristics
    purity
    wholesomeness
    efficacy
    accident risk
(d) Building Codes
(e) Health Services
    nursing homes
    private hospitals
    emergency services
(f) Animal Health
(g) Plant Health

Human Rights

Anti-discrimination legislation in respect to hiring, sale of goods or services etc.
Protection of privacy, personal information reporting

Labour

Collective bargaining
Minimum wage laws
Hours of work, terms of employment

Liquor

Characteristics, e.g., alcoholic content
Distribution and sale

Professions/ Occupational Licensure

Certification/Licensure
Registration
Apprenticeship

Transportation

Airlines (domestic, international)
Marine (domestic, international)
Railways
Inter-city Buses
Taxis
Pipelines
Trucking (inter and intra-provincial)
Urban Public Transit
Postal Express

Other

Rent control
Metrication
General wage and price controls

SOURCE   Economic Council of Canada (1979).

Changing Perspectives

It is now just over a decade since the Economic Council of Canada published its major report on government regulation.[3] A major focus of that study was the costs of direct regulation in a number of sectors of the economy. The Council believed that much direct regulation was unjustified, and that it imposed a significant burden on the economy. It has been estimated that 34 percent of Canadian GDP (excluding public administration and defence) was subject to price, output or entry control in 1980, when the Council was preparing its final report (Khemani 1985). Reforms introduced over the past decade have significantly reduced the scope as well as the stringency of such direct regulation. The most extensive process of reform has occurred in the transportation sector, but there has also been a relaxation of government regulation in the energy, telecommunications and, to a lesser extent, the finance sectors.

The Economic Council came to a more favourable conclusion in its assessment of social regulation. Although the Council had concerns about the process through which social regulations were being made, it considered the net effects of government activity in this area to be largely positive. Recently, social regulation has been viewed more critically. Recent concerns are linked, in part, to trade liberalization and the general movement towards the globalization of production. In this environment, social regulations that are relatively burdensome by international standards and that discourage trade and investment can entail substantial costs.[4]

Concern is also due to the perceived growth in social regulation. In the United States, such concern is supported by data on total regulatory costs assembled by Hopkins (1992). While regulatory reform resulted in a decline in total regulatory costs (measured in constant dollars) between 1977 and 1988, thereafter, the cost increases from new regulations, mostly in the environmental area, began to swamp the cost reductions from the elimination of direct regulation. In the absence of a similar measure of regulatory growth for Canada, it is useful to look at the data which are available on the pattern of government administrative costs. The data in Figure 1 suggest that, since the mid-1980s, there has been a significant redeployment of government resources from the administration of direct to the administration of social regulations. The emphasis in the Montreal seminar was on social, as opposed to direct regulation, with two of the papers focusing on the environmental area where there has been a particularly strong growth in real government spending (Figure 1).

With social regulation as with direct regulation, the fundamental question is whether government policies have enhanced the economic well-being of Canadians. The answer may be more problematic, however, because some benefits such as a cleaner environment, are not valued in the market. Studies that attempt to assess such regulations in terms of their impact on traditional market-based measures are therefore likely to be misleading. In a recent U.S. study involving a general equilibrium model, for example, the authors find that environmental regulation made a significant contribution to the decline in growth of the U.S. economy (Jorgenson and Wilcoxen 1990). However, a quite

Figure 1

Growth of federal and provincial government expenditure on regulatory activities, 1977-89

In percent per year and in constant dollars

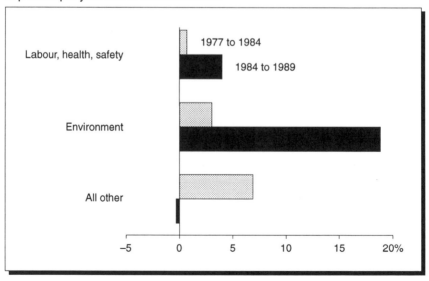

SOURCE   Based on S. Damus, *Canada's Public Sector: A Graphic Overview*, 1992.

different conclusion could be reached if growth were measured not by national accounts data, but by a more comprehensive measure that included an imputation for the benefits individuals derive from a cleaner environment. More generally, there is a need to be wary of aggregate measures purporting to show the cumulative impact and/or cost of government regulation. The economic well-being of Canadians is improved by those regulations that can pass a cost-benefit test in which all market and non-market impacts are properly evaluated.

Why Regulate? Market Failings

Traditionally, economists have found the rationale for regulation in the presence of certain conditions under which the market is unable to provide an efficient solution. Of course, the existence of a market failure is neither a necessary nor a sufficient condition for government intervention. It is not sufficient because governments, which are subject to their own "failures," may not be able to provide any more efficient solution than markets. It is not necessary because government intervention may be justified even if markets are perfectly efficient; while market outcomes may be efficient, they may involve wealth transfers that are unacceptable. As Ron Wintrobe and Robert Young remind us, governments must reconcile the requisites of growth with other societal demands, including security and fairness.

Still, where a market failure exists, where it entails significant costs, and where an alternative, less restrictive form of intervention is not available, regulation is, at least potentially, an attractive option. Regulation has been seen as a response to three main forms of market failure: natural monopoly, asymmetric information, and externalities.

In situations of natural monopoly — that is, where technology is such that market output is most efficiently provided by a single firm — government intervention to limit the exercise of market power can serve both efficiency and equity objectives. It is less clear than it used to be, however, what activities are natural monopolies. In recent years research has raised questions about the extent of economies of scale in a number of areas that were traditionally regarded as monopolies.

Where a monopoly does exist, the government can auction off the monopoly franchise instead of establishing a regulatory regime. A franchise arrangement is ostensibly appealing because it allows the benefits of competition to be realized; competition within a market is replaced by competition for the award of the franchise. But while franchise arrangements have worked well for activities such as urban mass transit and waste removal, they have been problematic where large amounts of long-lived specialized investment are required.[5] In the latter situation private investors require a long-term agreement commensurate with the long-term commitments they must make. Regulation is a type of implicit long-term contract that sets out the basic rights and obligations of the state and the owners of private capital. While regulation provides the parties with long-term stability, it also satisfies the need for flexibility by providing a procedure to resolve disputes and allow adjustments to be made over time to take account of changed economic circumstances and unforeseen contingencies. Regulation is, therefore, a seemingly reasonable way to address the contracting problems that occur where a monopoly arises from the need for highly durable, specialized assets.

Where information asymmetries are the problem, policies aimed at informing workers or consumers have intuitive appeal. The government could directly disseminate information, or subsidize private sector information providers. But information policies may be ineffective; workers and consumers may not notice or adequately digest the information. Individuals appear to have particular difficulty processing information about low probability hazards. Regulation may, therefore, provide a more effective and more appropriate response. In general, regulation is sensible in circumstances where the economies from delegating decision making to a third party (in this case the government) are likely to dominate the losses arising from the third party's inability to take account of the range of individual tastes.

Voluntary regulation is another alternative in markets where information asymmetries are a problem. In his paper, Empey discusses the role of voluntary standards organizations in setting product and process standards in the construction industry. Since these standards usually become incorporated in building codes and other regulations, the term "voluntary standards" is often a misnomer. Moreover, the concerns that Empey highlights with respect to the restrictive effect of voluntary standards on consumer choice and on competition are similar to concerns applying to government regulations. Voluntary standards — at least, those that are voluntary and not referenced in regulation — may offer certain advantages in terms of flexibility, but they are not necessarily less restrictive or less costly than regulation.

Externalities, the third form of market failure, arise where activities impose costs, or confer benefits, upon those not directly involved in the transaction. Environmental pollution, the classic externality, is discussed in the paper by Don Dewees. If a polluter does not pay for the damage his activities impose on third parties, the price of his output will not reflect the true costs of production. With a single polluter and a few pollution victims, there will be an incentive for the parties to come to an efficient arrangement. But most pollution problems involve a large number of parties and high transactions costs preclude negotiations. Tort law could force firms to internalize the costs of their pollution but, as Dewees points out, this rarely occurs in practice. The cost of legal redress is generally prohibitive, given the small loss incurred by each victim of pollution discharge. In addition, the existing degree of scientific uncertainty makes it difficult to prove liability and establish the appropriate amount of compensation. Hence, government intervention through regulation and/or taxation is necessary to prevent exploitation of the air, water and other common property resources.

Regulatory Failings

While there may be a role for regulation, there is reason to question whether and to what extent regulation is, in fact, being used to enhance the well-being of Canadians. In the United States, cost-benefit studies of federal regulation provide support for those who argue that regulation is a net burden on the economy. In a comprehensive review of the literature, for example, Hahn and Hird (1991) find that, on balance, direct regulation imposes an annual net cost on the economy of $46 billion (in 1988 dollars), while social regulation only generates benefits that are roughly equivalent to costs. While this suggests that the annual net costs of all regulations are less than one percent of U.S. GNP,

Table 2

Risks and Cost-Effectiveness of Selected Regulations (From the Budget for Fiscal Year 1992 – Table C-2, Part 2, p. 370)

Regulation[1]	Year issued	Health or safety?	Agency	Baseline mortality risk per million exposed	Cost per premature death averted ($ millions 1990)
Unvented Space Heater Ban	1980	S	CPSC	1,890	0.1
Aircraft Cabin Fire Protection Standard	1985	S	FAA	5	0.1
Auto Passive Restraint/Seat Belt Standards	1984	S	NHTSA	6,370	0.1
Steering Column Protection Standard[2]	1967	S	NHTSA	385	0.1
Underground Construction Standards[3]	1989	S	OSHA-S	38,700	0.1
Trihalomethane Drinking Water Standards	1979	H	EPA	420	0.2
Aircraft Seat Cushion Flammability Standard	1984	S	FAA	11	0.4
Alcohol and Drug Control Standards[3]	1985	H	FRA	81	0.4
Auto Fuel-System Integrity Standard	1975	S	NHTSA	343	0.4
Standards for Servicing Auto Wheel Rims[3]	1984	S	OSHA-S	630	0.4
Aircraft Floor Emergency Lighting Standard	1984	S	FAA	2	0.6
Concrete and Masonry Construction Standards[3]	1988	S	OSHA-S	630	0.6
Crane Suspended Personnel Platform Standard	1988	S	OSHA-S	81,000	0.7
Passive Restraints for Trucks and Buses (Proposed)	1989	S	NHTSA	6,370	0.7
Side-Impact Standards for Autos (Dynamic)	1990	S	NHTSA	n.a.	0.8
Children's Sleepwear Flammability Ban[4]	1973	S	CPSC	29	0.8
Auto Side Door Support Standards	1970	S	NHTSA	2,520	0.8
Low-Altitude Windshear Equipment and Training Standards	1988	S	FAA	n.a.	1.3
Electrical Equipment Standards (Metal Mines)	1970	S	MSHA	n.a.	1.4
Trenching and Excavation Standards[3]	1989	S	OSHA-S	14,310	1.5
Traffic Alert and Collision Avoidance (TCAS Systems)	1988	S	FAA	n.a.	1.5
Hazard Communication Standard[3]	1983	S	OSHA-S	1,800	1.6
Side-Impact Standards for Trucks, Buses, and MPVs (Proposed)	1989	S	NHTSA	n.a.	2.2
Grain Dust Explosion Prevention Standards[3]	1987	S	OSHA-S	9,450	2.8
Rear Lap/Shoulder Belts for Autos	1989	S	NHTSA	n.a.	3.2
Standards for Radionuclides in Uranium Mines[3]	1984	H	EPA	6,300	3.4
Benzene NESHAP (Original: Fugitive Emissions)	1984	H	EPA	1,470	3.4
Ethylene Dibromide Drinking Water Standard	1991	H	EPA	n.a.	5.7
Benzene NESHAP (Revised: Coke Byproducts)[3]	1988	H	EPA	n.a.	6.1
Asbestos Occupational Exposure Limit[3]	1972	H	OSHA-H	3,015	8.3

Table 2 (continued)

Regulation[1]	Year issued	Health or safety?	Agency	Baseline mortality risk per million exposed	Cost per premature death averted ($ millions 1990)
Benzene Occupational Exposure Limit[3]	1987	H	OSHA-H	39,600	8.9
Electrical Equipment Standards (Coal Mines)[3]	1970	S	MSHA	n.a.	9.2
Arsenic Emission Standards for Glass Plants	1986	H	EPA	2,660	13.5
Ethylene Oxide Occupational Exposure Limit[3]	1984	H	OSHA-H	1,980	20.5
Arsenic/Copper NESHAP	1986	H	EPA	63,000	23.0
Haz Waste Listing for Petroleum Refining Sludge	1990	H	EPA	210	27.6
Cover/Move Uranium Mill Tailings (Inactive Sites)	1983	H	EPA	30,100	31.7
Benzene NESHAP (Revised: Transfer Operations)	1990	H	EPA	n.a.	32.9
Cover/Move Uranium Mill Tailings (Active Sites)	1983	H	EPA	30,100	45.0
Acrylonitrile Occupational Exposure Limit[3]	1978	H	OSHA-H	42,300	51.5
Coke Ovens Occupational Exposure Limit[3]	1976	H	OSHA-H	7,200	63.5
Lockout/Tagout[3]	1989	S	OSHA-S	4	70.9
Asbestos Occupational Exposure Limit[3]	1986	H	OSHA-H	3,015	74.0
Arsenic Occupational Exposure Limit[3]	1978	H	OSHA-H	14,800	106.9
Asbestos Ban	1989	H	EPA	n.a.	110.7
Diethylstilbestrol (DES) Cattlefeed Ban	1979	H	FDA	22	124.8
Benzene NESHAP (Revised: Waste Operations)	1990	H	EPA	n.a.	168.2
1,2-Dichloropropane Drinking Water Standard	1991	H	EPA	n.a.	653.0
Haz Waste Land Disposal Ban (1st 3rd)	1988	H	EPA	2	4,190.4
Municipal Solid Waste Landfill Standards (Proposed)	1988	H	EPA	<1	19,107.0
Formaldehyde Occupational Exposure Limit[3]	1987	H	OSHA-H	31	86,201.8
Atrazine/Alachlor Drinking Water Standard	1991	H	EPA	n.a.	92,069.7
Haz Waste Listing for Wood-Preserving Chemicals	1990	H	EPA	<1	5,700,000.0

[1]70-year lifetime exposure assumed unless otherwise specified.
[2]50-year lifetime exposure.
[3]45-year lifetime exposure.
[4]12-year lifetime exposure.
n.a. – not available.
SOURCE: U.S. Office of Management and Budget (1992).

the authors believe that this is a significant underestimate of the regulatory burden. The estimate does not capture the adverse impact of many forms of regulation on innovation, nor does it reflect the increasing "drag" on the economy from the growth in social regulation. A review of U.S. health and safety regulations found that the costs of reducing risks were often extremely high (U.S. Office of Management and Budget 1992); in 21 of the 53 regulations examined the implicit cost of averting a premature death was over $10 million (see Table 2). A different allocation of these resources could have achieved a much greater reduction in societal risks. While there are no comparable overviews of Canadian regulation, assorted evidence calls into question the value of some regulatory programs, as well as various aspects of regulation making by federal and provincial governments.

As in the United States, the clearest evidence on the dead-weight loss from regulation is in the area of direct regulation. The economic losses associated with supply marketing boards in poultry and dairy were a major focus of concern in the Economic Council study, and these concerns remain relevant.[6] In telecommunications, there has been some significant regulatory reform, but there is evidence that the current regulatory regime has entailed substantial costs; Globerman (1991), for example, estimates that the dead-weight loss arising from the cross-subsidy of local telephone service by long-distance service has been over $2 billion (1984 dollars) per year.[7] The costs of regulating transport carriers in inherently competitive industries are well documented. (See Wilson 1992; and Hahn and Hird 1991.) This literature is relevant to the continued regulation of intercity busing, intraprovincial trucking in some provinces, and taxi operations in most major municipalities.

While there is general acceptance of the objectives of health and safety regulation, concerns have been raised about the stringency of some requirements. The Commission of Inquiry on the Pharmaceutical Industry (the Eastman Commission), for example, believed that the regulatory delay in the certification of new drugs resulted in "beneficial drugs ... (being) introduced later than necessary, thus depriving patients of potential aid." (Eastman Commission 1986, p. xxv.) The efficiency with which resources have been allocated to risk reduction has been reduced by the use of very different values for death avoidance in regulatory assessments. There is a wide variation even within individual federal departments. For example, Transport Canada has used values varying from $310,000 in road safety to as high as $2.9 million (1989 dollars) in some aviation investment evaluations.[8] In occupational health and safety, Canada appears to have avoided some of the heavy costs that characterize federal regulation in the United States through a decentralized approach in which reliance is placed on work site employer-employee committees to determine health and safety requirements. But concerns have been raised about the influence of Workers' Compensation on employers' incentive to prevent accidents (Rea 1983). Research has also questioned the effectiveness of provincial regulations. A recent study, for example, failed to establish a clear relationship between provincial regulations and the frequency and severity of workplace accidents in Quebec over the 1982-87 period (Lanoie 1989).

These examples of inappropriate and poorly designed policies can be traced to a number of sources of "regulatory failure." First, there is the role of political considerations. The objectives of those with influence on government policy do not correspond perfectly with the requirements for efficiency. Second, there are the information problems confronting government regulators. Due to information problems, efficient regulation would be very difficult even if governments were entirely motivated by public interest considerations. Third, there is the complication arising from institutional factors. The allocation of responsibilities among departments and among governments in Canada is a further impediment to efficient regulation.

Political and Bureaucratic Considerations

To some observers, it is not surprising that regulation may reduce economic welfare since the regulatory agenda is primarily shaped by well-organized groups whose primary objective is to increase their member's wealth, rather than national wealth. According to this view, the primary beneficiaries of regulation are narrowly-based groups whose members each have much to gain from successful political action. The costs of regulation, on the other hand, are widely dispersed, thereby making the costs of organizing effective political opposition prohibitive.[9]

The notion that regulation is a mechanism for transferring wealth to well-organized groups appears to explain some outcomes that are difficult to reconcile with the view that regulation exists to remedy market failures. But it is not consistent with a number of regulatory and regulatory reform initiatives that seem primarily to serve the interests of broadly-based groups.[10] Moreover, there is always a danger in interpreting behaviour based on knowledge that is gained *ex post*. Regulations that diminish national wealth may have been motivated by a legitimate concern for the public interest. That the public interest is sometimes difficult to identify was illustrated by the discussion of labour market regulation at the seminar. Morley Gunderson pointed out that labour regulations designed to provide more equitable outcomes often have adverse incentive effects that undermine efficiency. On the other hand, in their presentation Wintrobe and Young showed how measures to somewhat improve the relative position of workers in the secondary labour market can increase what they call "social efficiency," a measure that not only captures worker productivity, but also the economic losses that are a product of worker frustration and alienation.

Special interest theories of regulation provide some useful insights, but they do not offer the only, nor necessarily the most important explanation, for regulatory failure. The root of the "political problem" is that the key decisionmakers — politicians, government officials, and members of regulatory boards — are agents with interests that are likely to diverge, to at least some extent, from the broader public interest. Decisionmakers may be able to advance their self-interest by conferring benefits on well-organized groups,[11] or by according favourable treatment to firms subject to regulation.[12] Alternatively, they may see their interest in the growth of their area of regulatory activity.[13] Or politicians and officials may view their prospects as being tied to their ability to satisfy public perceptions and expectations, as uninformed as these may be.[14] The influence of these and other personal and organizational considerations on regulation making in Canada is open to debate. What is significant, however, is that such political influences do exist and that, as a result, regulation is not designed solely with a view to maximizing social welfare.

Information Problems

Even if government's only objective were to maximize social welfare, this would be exceedingly difficult to achieve because of information problems. The seminar provided a number of insights into this form of regulatory failure.

Direct Regulation

As Boyer notes, the regulator administering a system of rate-of-return regulation faces a principal-agent problem analogous to that confronting firm owners who have delegated management responsibilities and must ensure these are being diligently performed. The problem is also similar to that faced by the public at large vis-à-vis government. To determine revenue requirements of, say, a utility, regulators must establish what is required to cover operating cost and provide an adequate return on capital. Where regulators are concerned about the pricing structure of utility services, they must also look at costs and how the firm has chosen to allocate fixed costs among its outputs. If regulators dared to try a more theoretically optimal pricing scheme — i.e., Ramsey-Boiteux pricing[15] — they would require detailed information on the cost and demand function for individual products. Whatever approach is adopted, the regulatory board is highly dependent on the data provided by the utility itself. The regulator will generally not have access to alternative information which can serve as a "yardstick" to assess the reasonableness of the results being reported.

Boyer notes that allowed rates of return are generally set higher than regulated firms' cost of capital, thereby encouraging producers to overcapitalize (the Averch-Johnson effect). Under rate-of-return regulation, there is also considerable scope for organizational inefficiency. The regulatory board may attempt to review costs to ensure they do not reflect waste and inefficiency, but, as Boyer points out, it has little practical alternative but to accept the data provided by the firm. The board again faces major difficulties when it comes to determining if the firm is appropriately installing new capital equipment that will allow its customers to benefit from lower costs and/or improved service.

Information problems are even more complex when direct regulation is applied to industries with more than one participant. In telecommunications, for example, the regulatory task has been complicated by the participation of some firms in both competitive and monopolistic activities. Regulators have had to try to ensure that monopoly services are not carrying an excessive share of the firms' common costs and thereby subsidizing competitive services. In transportation, direct regulation has often included efforts to exercise control over entry, rates, equipment and the service provided by large numbers of carriers. George Wilson (1992, p. 292) has aptly described the resulting problem:

> Even single-firm monopoly cannot be regulated in terms of allowable rates of return without unwanted side effects such as inefficient production, expense padding and other aspects of the so-called A-J-W effect. How much more complex it is to seek to regulate dozens or even hundreds of thousands of firms ... with their varying cost and service characteristics, different capital intensities and other special features. The attempt to regulate such a hodge-podge is bound to fail if the objective is efficiency or the achievement of non-economic goals at least cost and the maintenance of some spirit of enterprise and risk-taking.

Environmental Regulation

A policy that optimally controls pollutants would result in the elimination of discharges up to the point where the costs of abatement just equal the gains from reduced emissions. But, as Dewees discusses, there is much scientific uncertainty about the harm caused by various pollutants and the benefits of reducing exposure. Even with respect to air pollution, which has been monitored for many years, there is conflicting scientific evidence on the nature and severity of health effects. The uncertainty is greater for the numerous substances that may be acutely toxic. Reliable information on dose-response relationships exists for only a small number of the thousands of toxic substances that may warrant some regulatory control.

There are some additional factors that complicate the assessment of gains from pollution control. One is the spatial factor; the harm caused by some emissions varies considerably by location.

The effects of acid rain, for example, are greater when the natural buffering capacity of the local ecosystem has been exceeded. There are also intertemporal considerations; the benefits of pollution control will partly accrue to future generations. Some environmentalists have questioned the use of discount rates that have the effect of trivializing very long-term benefits. But the application of abnormally low discount rates to environmental investment will discriminate against other forms of wealth creation that could yield greater benefits for future generations.

Optimal pollution abatement requires a sensitivity to costs as well as benefits. While individual producers know their own cost functions, the government must generally work with information on the costs of the representative producer or the representative producer in a particular class (for example, the class of existing versus the class of new firms). With government establishing discharge limits, therefore, it is not possible to arrive at the optimal solution where all firms that are discharging a particular pollutant face the same marginal costs of abatement.

In practice, governments have not tried to fine-tune their regulations to approximate the results of cost-benefit calculations. They have, however, opted for detailed emission standards that still make enormous information-gathering demands on those designing and enforcing the regulations. For example, Ontario's MISA program, which is aimed at controlling discharges of toxic substances into waterways, and its CAP program, which targets certain forms of air pollution, adopt technology-based standards. Under MISA, the Ontario government will set discharge limits by pollutant and by sector, based on the "best available technology that is economically achievable." The implementation of MISA and CAP is in itself a formidable challenge. Dewees suggests that "either the careful and detailed consideration outlined in the draft (CAP) regulation will be abandoned in favour of simple processes, such as adopting U.S. standards, or the regulatory process will require years and enormous manpower to complete."

Health and Safety Regulation

In regulating health and safety, as in regulating the environment, standards would ideally be set so as to maximize net benefits. Information problems again make this extremely difficult to achieve. On the benefit side there are a number of sources of uncertainty. As a result of scientific disputes about the harm from exposure to a number of chemical substances, benefit estimates may here again be subject to a wide margin of error. The cause of accidents in the workplace and in the home is often unclear. Hence the safety benefits from changes in product design or new production techniques may be uncertain. Moreover, regulations may have unintended side effects. Standards that discourage the consumption of a particular food product, for example, could lead consumers to purchase more of another product that poses even more serious long-term risks. Compliance with occupational health and safety requirements may require the use of an untested production technology that poses new and unanticipated risks.

The estimation of benefits also involves difficult evaluation problems. There is no generally accepted value for reducing fatalities or eliminating pain and hardship. Moreover, individual workers and consumers are likely to attach different values to the benefits of risk reduction. A regulation that eliminates lower quality and somewhat more hazardous products from the market may deny some consumers their preferred choices.

The estimation of the costs of complying with health and safety standards must take account not only of direct outlays on machinery and equipment, but also the effect of required operating changes on productivity. In the case of occupational health and safety regulation, costs of compliance are likely to vary considerably across industries and across plants. While an optimal approach would attempt to equalize the marginal costs of achieving a given improvement, this flexibility is difficult to achieve with a centralized administrative approach. Studies of the U.S. Occupational Safety and Health Administration (OSHA) have been highly critical of the agency's tendency to apply the same standard to all industries, irrespective of costs.[16]

The costs of health and safety regulation include government inspection and enforcement costs. Concerns that have arisen suggest that, in some areas, governments have underestimated the resources required for effective enforcement of health and safety regulations. Information problems in this area relate in part to the difficulty of predicting market changes. Over time, the enforcement function of government will change as changes occur in production technology, the number of domestic producers, and the quantity of imports.

Institutional Factors

Existing institutional arrangements are another major impediment to optimal regulation. The allocation of regulatory responsibilities among governments and between government departments can result in duplication and conflict that greatly increase regulatory costs. These problems could be avoided if regulatory authorities could coordinate and harmonize their policies,[17] but the establishment of adequate institutional arrangements has proved to be a difficult challenge.

A major concern to industry is the perceived overlap and duplication in the regulatory activities of governments. Private sector managers view regulatory overlap as a significant source of added costs. Governments have, in fact, attempted to eliminate the most serious problems of overlap by reshuffling responsibilities and establishing coordinating mechanisms. At the seminar, for example, George Kowalski noted that the *Canadian Environmental Protection Act* included two mechanisms to facilitate cooperative implementation of national standards: equivalency agreements, which suspend the operation of a federal regulation where a provincial regulation exists, and administrative agreements, which provide for shared administration of CEPA. Mechanisms have also been established to prevent overlap among departmental activities. For example, Memoranda of Understanding between the federal departments that regulate food products (Agriculture Canada, Consumer and Corporate Affairs, Health and Welfare, and Fisheries) attempt to clarify roles and responsibilities and establish a single contact point for industries and consumers. Such initiatives have not significantly allayed private sector concerns.[18] However, the most serious problem may not be duplication — i.e., that exactly the same activity is being regulated by two or more departments or governments — but the failure of officials to take account of the full impact of the regulation imposed by different governments, and different departments on particular firms and sectors.

The nature of the burden that can result from the cumulative activities of different regulatory bodies was illustrated by Empey's paper on the non-residential construction industry. Contractors, engineers and architects are subject to a wide range of federal, local and provincial laws, which are given expression through a complex maze of codes and standards. Empey believes the high costs of achieving current standards has discouraged new construction, although (as Frank Clayton points out) it is not clear that the situation is worse in Canadian than in U.S. cities.

Neufeld's paper on environmental assessment also pointed to some concerns about the cumulative impact of government regulatory processes. Both federal and provincial governments conduct environmental assessments, and municipalities are considering their use. From his survey Neufeld did not find evidence that environmental assessments are adversely affecting Canada's competitive position. However, he did find that environmental assessments carried out by different government departments and agencies, and the ability of intervenors to "bump up" provincial assessments that were well underway to the federal level, were adding significantly to the cost and complexity of this form of regulation.

The lack of adequate coordination between federal and provincial governments is, arguably, of less consequence than the failure to fully harmonize provincial standards. Different provincial occupational and professional licensing requirements, and different provincial product standards are a barrier to the free movement of labour and goods. They limit the gains available to producers and consumers from participating in a national, as opposed to a smaller provincial, market. The resulting losses may be offset — but probably only marginally — by the benefits from experimenting with different regulatory regimes.

In many areas of activity, however, it is not feasible to establish "regulatory walls," and in these areas provinces are under pressure to harmonize their standards to attract capital and business. Gunderson contends that "leading edge" labour regulations (i.e., hours of work, paid holidays, vacation and parental leave) and regulations to promote equity will increasingly be constrained by economic forces. The pressure to move to the lowest common denominator may induce jurisdictions to agree to a common set of principles, thus enabling labour equity objectives to be satisfied.

Regulatory Reform

When regulation is not improving the welfare of Canadians, the main options are to eliminate it — and thereby rely either on market forces or an alternative policy instrument — or to substantially improve regulatory design, administration and enforcement. There was some discussion of deregulation at the seminar, but the major focus was on the prospects for improving regulation through the use of market-based incentives.

Deregulation

For Boyer, deregulation is the first reform option that should be considered. He advocates the elimination of direct regulation where this has been made possible by technological change or changes in national and international competition. Both factors have, in fact, already contributed to liberalization in a number of areas.

Telecommunication has been subject to rapid technological change, which has placed in doubt the need for monopoly provision of many telecommunications services. The recent decision by the CRTC to allow competition in long-distance telephone service was a recognition of the changed technology of telephone service, and also a response to the threat posed by the increasing diversion of Canadian long-distance traffic over U.S. networks. (See Sherman 1992.) The significant deregulation of transportation which occurred in 1987 was prompted partly by the desire to put Canadian carriers on an equal footing with their deregulated U.S. counterparts. Transport reforms were based, as well, on a recognition of the importance of an efficient transportation system to Canada's ability to compete in world markets. In financial services, international developments have also exerted pressures for the reform of Canada's regulatory policies. While the government has not succeeded in passing a comprehensive reform program, regulatory changes at the federal and provincial level have greatly increased competition in the securities industry.

Deregulation is desirable where there is no longer a valid rationale for government intervention, or where public policy objectives can be addressed by an alternative, less restrictive and less costly form of intervention. Canada's experience provides some substantiation of the benefits of deregulation, although that experience is limited, both in scope and duration. Moreover, it is difficult to isolate the impact of regulatory reforms from other factors, including the recent prolonged weakness in the overall economy.

If we look, for example, at the transportation sector, we can find various indications of a more competitive environment. Provisions in the *National Transportation Act* (NTA), 1987, which abolished railways' rights to set rates collectively and allowed railways and shippers to enter into confidential contracts, have promoted competition among the railways in a number of markets (National Transportation Agency 1991). Shippers report that confidential contracting has helped them secure lower rates and competitive terms of service. In extra-provincial trucking, increased competition has resulted from the relaxation in entry restrictions in the *Motor Vehicle Transportation Act*, 1987. The results are reflected not only in rates, but also in the pressures for a consolidation and rationalization of trucking services (National Transportation Agency 1991). Efficiency should increase as carriers redesign their routes and otherwise adjust their activities to take advantage of available marketing and operating economies.

In the airline industry, it is particularly difficult to distinguish the effects of regulatory reform from that of the economic downturn and other events that have increased industry costs and reduced revenues. However, in the period from 1984, when regulation began to be significantly relaxed, until 1991 there were some important changes in the industry. In Canada, as in the United States, the relaxation of regulatory control allowed the major carriers to reorganize and rationalize their operations. One result has been the trend towards "hub-and-spoke" routing systems whereby passengers are routed through a central location from which they take connecting flights to their final destination. Another result has been the reallocation of routes among carriers; smaller markets have been transferred by the majors to their affiliates which can offer service using more appropriate aircraft. The efficiency gains resulting from these developments were reflected partly in the increase in scheduled airline service; travellers benefited from increased frequency of service and service to more locations (National Transportation Agency 1991; and Hirshhorn 1992).

Although competition in individual airline markets increased over the period 1984 to 1991, the high level of concentration in the industry has been a concern. Contrary to expectations of the proponents of deregulation, airline markets are not perfectly contestable; the threat of entry is a weak disciplining mechanism for major carriers who have a number of important advantages over potential entrants (i.e., their ownership of computer reservation systems, their frequent flier programs, their control over feeder systems, and, sometimes, their rights to scarce airport slots and gates) (Acheson and McFetridge 1992; and Hirshhorn 1992). This is of greater concern in Canada than in the United States where the degree of actual (as distinct from potential) competition in most markets is adequate. In Canada, the tenuous state of competition does not suggest that regulatory reform was a mistake. It does point to the importance of government policies aimed at reducing barriers to entry into airline markets. It also raises questions about the desirability of those regulatory barriers to entry that continue to apply to foreign investors and foreign airlines.

Improving Regulation Through the Use of Market-Based Incentives[19]

Direct Regulation

There is a growing literature on the principal-agent problems that complicate the regulation of monopolies. Many of the theoretical solutions devised by economists, however, are politically impractical or technically unfeasible. Under the Loeb-Magat scheme discussed in Boyer's paper, regulated monopolists are induced to price efficiently and to minimize costs by the provision of a subsidy equal to the amount of consumer surplus. As Green points out in his comments, even if this scheme could be made politically acceptable, it is a "non-starter" because the requisite information on cost and demand functions is so difficult to obtain.

"Price-cap" regulation, by contrast, has minimal information requirements. The firm is allowed to increase prices according to a formula based on the inflation rate, minus an X factor that is intended to reflect anticipated productivity gains due to technological change. Price-cap regulation is popular in the U.K. where it was developed and is gaining increased attention among North American regulators. Price-cap regulation has appeal because of its relative simplicity and the explicit incentives it provides for cost efficiency. But the evidence is not yet in as to whether, over the longer term, it produces superior results to rate-of-return regulation. As Boyer points out, there is an incentive for firms to behave opportunistically every four to five years as the time for review of the formula approaches. In particular, the firm will want to avoid giving the impression of being too successful, since the regulator could react by substantially increasing X and thereby making the firm's life more difficult over the period to the next review. Moreover, as Green noted, so long as regulators focus on controlling prices (as opposed to the return on capital) under rate-of-return regulation, this also incorporates incentives for cost reduction.

Nonetheless, the general view at the seminar was that price-cap regulation holds promise, particularly if it is combined with a "yardstick" measure, as proposed by Boyer. With a suitable price index and a yardstick tying X to productivity gains in other industries or to the same industry in other countries, regulatory reviews could be less frequent and the adverse incentives associated with such reviews could be minimized.

Environmental Regulation

The potential gains from adopting market incentives in place of existing command-and-control mechanisms in environmental regulation are discussed by Dewees. The primary incentive mechanisms are an effluent charge (EC), which is a tax on each unit of pollution discharged, and marketable pollution permits (MPPs), which are rights to discharge a given amount of a pollutant in a given region.[20] These mechanisms do not resolve all the information problems discussed above. Governments still face the problem of identifying what pollutants to control and determining how stringently to control each type of discharge. But they can reduce the costs of achieving a given level of environmental protection. Effluent charges and marketable permits will lead to the cost-minimizing outcome where all firms discharging a given pollutant face the same marginal cost of abatement.

Dewees discusses some important additional advantages of market mechanisms. They provide incentives for technological progress since with both an EC and MPPs there are clear gains available to firms that can improve pollution control. Under the traditional approach, firms that fail to comply with standards face minor costs. Market approaches will also cause market prices to incorporate pollution costs. Resource allocation will be improved as product prices thereby come to reflect the true costs of production. MPPs have the further advantage that they require less information and can be more speedily implemented than technology-based programs such as MISA and CAP in Ontario.

The federal government and the provinces have been exploring the possibility of using market incentives to help control sulphur dioxide emissions, and to address ozone problems resulting from emissions of nitrogen oxide and volatile organic compounds. Dewees believes that market incentives can also improve the cost-effectiveness of other regulatory programs, including those based on best-available technology, those aimed at controlling some toxic emissions, and those aimed at fulfilling Canada's commitment to the reduction of greenhouse gases.

Other Areas

The possibility of improving regulation through market incentives was also broached in the papers by Gunderson and Empey. Gunderson suggests that labour market regulation would be improved if regulators took greater account of the preferences of workers as expressed through the collective bargaining process. In particular, regulators should question why desired changes have not been introduced through collective bargaining. Gunderson raises the possibility of exempting collective agreements that meet basic procedural requirements from certain regulatory provisions. This would prevent regulation from overturning arrangements that reasonably well-informed private parties have freely negotiated.

The current emphasis in labour market regulation is on preventing socially undesirable outcomes. Gunderson points to a number of areas where it would be preferable to influence incentives and allow workers and employers to determine the appropriate response. For example: instead of regulating maximum working hours, employers can be required to pay a specified premium for overtime work; efforts can be made to internalize the third party costs of public sector strikes through tax rebates for services not provided; and experience rating can be introduced under Workers' Compensation, so that employers will more directly bear the cost of a failure to provide safe working conditions.

Empey discusses how market incentives could be accorded a greater role by moving from prescriptive to performance-based standards. While Empey's focus is on construction and building product standards, the issue is relevant to social regulation in general. Whereas prescriptive or design standards specify precise requirements, performance standards establish objectives (usually in terms of a specified test) that must be satisfied and leave managers free to determine the best way to achieve the desired result. A major advantage of performance standards is that, unlike design standards, they are conducive to innovation. Performance standards tend to be more costly to monitor and enforce than prescriptive standards, but this cost is often more than offset by the benefits from providing producers with incentives that promote economic efficiency.

Pressure and Process

From this brief overview, we are left with a problem and a question. The problem arises because markets provide a highly unsatisfactory solution under some conditions; because regulation is, in some of these circumstances, the most appropriate form of intervention; and because the results of using regulation have been disappointing in many respects. The question is: What can be done to improve the situation?

The logical point of focus is the regulation-making process within government. Can the establishment of new mechanisms and the reform of regulation-making processes contribute to more efficient regulation? In particular, is it possible to generate pressures for the elimination of unnecessary and undesirable regulations, for a more thorough consideration of the possibilities for employing less restrictive forms of government intervention, and for the adoption of market-based incentives that offer the prospect of more cost-effective regulation?

In addressing these questions, we must recognize the limitations of our understanding about why and how governments intervene. There is no generally accepted theory about why governments regulate and deregulate. Since it is difficult to discriminate among alternative models of political and bureaucratic behaviour, there will necessarily be some uncertainty as to whether, and to what extent, proposed reforms will contribute to the desired decision-making incentives.

Some researchers would take the view that "institutional tinkering" cannot influence the broader forces shaping the political agenda. They would contend that politically influential groups will be able to turn any new institutional arrangements or processes towards the achievement of their own objectives. They would argue that important regulatory changes have been a result not of process changes, but of changes in the economic environment that have undermined the usefulness of regulation as a mechanism for transferring wealth (Peltzman 1989).

Even if this accurately depicted the situation, we could not conclude that regulatory mechanisms and processes are unimportant. Individuals care about the way decisions are made.

Decision-making processes that are just and credible are valuable in their own right. Hence, measures to promote transparency and improve accountability are important, quite aside from whatever influence they may have on the decision-making outcomes.

However, it may be a mistake to dismiss the potential influence of the regulatory process on decision-making outcomes. Process changes can affect the incentives of politicians and public officials. More rigorous analysis combined with greater transparency should increase the political costs of "bad regulation," that is, regulation that clearly diminishes our collective wealth. The notion that "ideas matter" and that an informed electorate can be a force for more efficient regulation is supported by some of the literature examining recent deregulation.[21] It is also consistent with the evidence that policymakers are influenced by public perceptions. An informed public should be concerned about the high cost of standards that are significantly more stringent than those of our trading partners; sensitive to the potential for reducing fatalities by more efficiently allocating regulatory resources devoted to risk reduction; and, open to the contribution economic incentives can make to more cost-effective pollution control.

The regulatory process can also be used to reduce biases that may lead politicians to favour regulation over alternative instruments. Regulation is appealing in some circumstances, for example, because it allows "hidden" or implicit transfers from one group to another. Measures that make the income transfers resulting from regulation more visible might be expected to reduce its attractiveness relative to instruments involving explicit transfers. Another appealing feature of regulation, especially at a time of budgetary restraint, is that regulatory costs are largely off-budget. The establishment of a "regulatory budget," which puts a ceiling on annual public and private sector regulatory costs, could redress the resulting imbalance between regulation and other policy instruments.

All this suggests that the most important reforms are likely to be those that will contribute to more rigorous analysis of existing and proposed regulations, and that will lead to greater transparency. The administrative procedures introduced by the government in 1986 to promote more systematic regulatory analysis and greater consultation were a useful start, but the process can be considerably strengthened. An examination of a sample of Regulatory Impact Analysis Statements (RIAS) completed in 1991 generally confirmed what others have found, namely that the rigor of regulatory impact analyses leaves much to be desired. (See, e.g., Zafiriou 1992.) This review also highlighted the point that many new regulations consist of fairly minor "housekeeping" measures. More efficient regulation depends not just on the careful scrutiny of new regulations, but also on a commitment to periodically review the stock of existing regulations.

There are a number of reforms that could impose increased discipline on the regulatory process, and improve the accountability of decisionmakers. First, there are the proposals that have been put forward to limit the growth in regulations through the establishment of a regulatory budget. The intention would be to establish a ceiling on total regulatory costs akin to the ceiling on spending that is imposed by the fiscal budget. There are difficulties in identifying and assembling the required data on total regulatory costs, and while research undertaken in the United States suggests these problems are amenable to reasonable solutions, (e.g., Hopkins 1992; and Morrall 1991) implementation questions require further investigation. It should be recognized, however, that even an imperfect set of accounts could be effective in "rationing" the use of regulation, and forcing policymakers to make trade-offs similar to those that must be made with policies involving government spending.

Second, sunset clauses could be incorporated in major regulations. This would ensure that such regulations are periodically reviewed in the context of changing economic conditions and changing government objectives. While departments have been asked to review their regulatory programs at least once every seven years, this objective has not been met. Sunset clauses could inject some needed discipline along with a useful sense of urgency into the review exercise.

Third, there could be merit in centralizing responsibility for the evaluation of major regulations. At the federal level, the preparation of major RIASs could be delegated to specialists within Treasury Board in the same way that the drafting of regulations is assigned to specialized Department of Justice lawyers. This would give recognition to the specialized expertise required for regulatory analysis and would help to ensure that RIASs adhere to a common approach and satisfy a uniform standard of analysis. There are also certain benefits from placing responsibility for evaluating regulations with a department that is not as directly involved with stakeholders, and that has no organizational interest to promote as the administrator and enforcer of the regulation. While Treasury Board analysts would have to draw on the specialized knowledge of officials in the regulating department, such cooperation should not be a problem. A separation in functions, however, could make it more difficult to coordinate the regulatory analysis with public consultations and ensure that these exercises are mutually reinforcing.

Finally, it may be desirable to encourage independent regulatory assessments by researchers outside government. Such research would provide legislatures and the public with an alternative source of information to that provided by the government itself. The most direct way to foster independent research is to establish an independent agency devoted to the review of existing and proposed government regulations. Boyer proposes that such an agency be created to carry out an independent assessment of existing regulatory regimes and also to design mechanisms that will ease the transition from a protected to a market-oriented environment. As an alternative to the establishment of a new agency, support could be provided to existing institutions that are directing their research at regulatory questions of policy interest. Whichever route is chosen, it is important that the supported research is relevant to the public policy debate, and that it is indeed independent. There is perhaps a role here for federal and provincial legislative committees. They could serve as sources of independent funding for research on regulatory issues, and ensure that such research is available in time to make a contribution to their own deliberations and to the overall public policy debate.

While the call for increased resources to be devoted to regulatory analysis appears to run counter to the thrust of current budgetary pressures, a more critical approach should have, on balance, a favourable impact on government finances. Significant savings should be achieved as the federal government is relieved of the burden of administering unnecessary and undesirable regulations.

The above proposals, however, should be seen in the context of broader efforts to strengthen the accountability of public sector decisionmakers. Government regulation will continue to play an important role in coming years in responding to environmental problems and other social concerns. At a time when firms are under increased pressure to become internationally competitive, governments must be vigilant in ensuring that regulation is being employed in the appropriate circumstances and in the appropriate way. An informed public is likely to provide the best prospect for a vigilant and responsible public sector.

Acknowledgements

We benefited from the comments on a previous draft from Judith Maxwell, Bryne Purchase, Ron Crowley, Jim Martin and Basil Zafiriou. Responsibility for the views expressed in this paper, of course, rests entirely with the authors.

Notes

1. Most regulations are contained in legislation that is subordinate to, or delegated by, a federal or provincial Act. Our definition, however, would include the rules incorporated in regulatory Acts themselves as well as the rules contained in delegated legislation.

2. This is based on unpublished data collected by Treasury Board. The number excludes public officials involved in the administration and enforcement of Canada's tax regulations. The addition of this latter group would raise the total number of employees associated with federal regulatory activity to over 80,000.

3. See Economic Council of Canada, *Reforming Regulation*. Recommendations were also contained in the interim report, *Responsible Regulation*.

4. Relatively stringent standards may be an import barrier and an impediment to exports. Canadian firms may have to manufacture a distinctive product to comply with foreign regulations or to be cost competitive in foreign markets with less demanding requirements. If Canadian regulations were to significantly reduce our overall

competitiveness, the cost may be borne by Canadians through a decline in the purchasing power of their currency in foreign markets.

5. This discussion draws on H. Demsetz, "Why Regulate Utilities?" and O. Williamson, "Franchise Bidding for Natural Monopolies: In General and with respect to CATV."

6. The major Council study was J.D. Forbes, R.D. Hughes and T.K. Warley, "Economic Intervention and Regulation in Canadian Agriculture." More recent studies include G.C. Van Kooten and J. Spriggs, "A Comparative Static Analysis of the Welfare Impacts of Supply Restricting Marketing Boards," and M.M. Veeman, "Marketing Boards: the Canadian Experience."

7. These costs should decline as the effects of the recent decision to allow competition in long distance telephone service work their way through the system.

8. Different values may be appropriate if they reflect the different values individuals attach to reducing different forms of risk. In 1992, a single value of $1.5 million was adopted by Transport Canada for death avoidance. See Royal Commission on National Passenger Transportation, *Final Report*, vol. 2, p. 283.

9. The reference is to the "Chicago theories" developed by G. Stigler, "The Theory of Economic Regulation," S. Peltzman, "Toward a More General Theory of Regulation," and G. Becker, "Public Policies, Pressure Groups and Deadweight Costs."

10. See S. Peltzman, "The Economic Theory of Regulation after a Decade of Deregulation," and R. Noll, "Discussion of Peltzman paper." The application to Canada is discussed by D.G. McFetridge and A. Lall, "Is There a Theory of Deregulation?"

11. As discussed in G. Stigler, "The Theory of Economic Regulation."

12. As discussed by "capture" theories of regulation. See, for example, R.D. Eckert, "Spectrum Allocation and Regulatory Incentives."

13. The reference here is to the work of economists such as Niskanen who allege that it is the bureaucracy that benefits from being able to exercise control over the coercive power of the state.

14. Regulations that involve an extremely high cost per premature death avoided may, in part, be the result of government efforts to satisfy public concerns based on inaccurate risk perceptions.

15. Ramsey-Boiteux pricing gives recognition to the need for firms with declining long-run average costs to set prices in excess of average (as well as marginal) costs to break even. The objective of the pricing scheme is to minimize the welfare losses arising from the need to depart from an optimal pricing scheme based on marginal costs. As Boyer notes, in Ramsey-Boiteux pricing, prices are marked up above marginal costs (to the extent required to achieve break even) with the percentage mark-up for each product being inversely related to the elasticity of demand.

16. Critical assessments of OSHA include J. Mendeloff, *Regulating Safety: An Economic and Political Analysis of Occupational Safety and Health Policy*; W.K. Viscusi, "The Impact of Occupational Safety and Health Regulation, 1973-1983," and A.P. Bartel and L.G. Thomas, "Direct and Indirect Effects of Regulation: A New Look at OSHA's Impact."

17. Efforts to coordinate and harmonize government policies, however, can in themselves absorb significant economic resources.

18. This is apparent from the submissions received by the House of Commons Standing Committee on Finance in their recent inquiry into regulation and competitiveness. See B. Zafiriou, "Inquiry into Regulation and Competitiveness: Summary of Evidence Received."

19. The challenge of establishing incentives for the efficient provision of government programs and services was addressed in a number of seminars held by the Government and Competitiveness Project. Of relevance are the forthcoming G&C publications, *Efficient Program Delivery, Efficient Purchasing*, and *Efficient Policy*.

20. While subsidies have received less attention in the literature, in some circumstances they may be the most appropriate form of market-based incentive. This is discussed in J. Pezzey, "The Symmetry Between Controlling Pollution by Price and Controlling it by Quantity."

21. This is discussed in D.G. McFetridge and A. Lall, "Is There a Theory of Deregulation?"

References

Acheson, K. and D. McFetridge. 1992. Controlling Market Power in Weakly Contestable Canadian Airline Markets. In Royal Commission on National Passenger Transportation, *Final Report* vol. 3.

Bartel, A.P. and L.G. Thomas. 1985. Direct and Indirect Effects of Regulation: A New Look at OSHA's Impact. *Journal of Law and Economics* 27.

Becker, G. 1985. Public Policies, Pressure Groups and Deadweight Costs. *Journal of Public Economics* 28.

Commission of Inquiry on the Pharmaceutical Industry (Eastman Commission) 1986. *Report*. Ottawa: Supply and Services Canada.

Damus, S. 1992. *Canada's Public Sector*. Economic Council of Canada. Ottawa: Supply and Services Canada.

Demsetz, H. 1968. Why Regulate Utilities? *Journal of Law and Economics* 11.

Eckert R.D. 1972. Spectrum Allocation and Regulatory Incentives. In *Conference on Communications Policy: Papers and Proceedings*. Washington, DC: Office of Telecommunications Policy.

Economic Council of Canada. 1979. *Responsible Regulation*. Ottawa: Supply and Services Canada.

_____. 1981. *Reforming Regulation*. Ottawa: Supply and Services Canada.

Forbes, J.D., R.D. Hughes, and T.K. Warley. 1982. Economic Intervention and Regulation in Canadian Agriculture. Ottawa: Economic Council of Canada.

Globerman, S. 1991. Deregulation of Telecommunications: An Assessment. In Block and Lermer, eds. *Breaking the Shackles: Deregulating Canadian Industry*. Vancouver: The Fraser Institute.

Hahn R.W. and J.A. Hird. 1991. The Costs and Benefits of Regulation: Review and Synthesis. *Yale Journal on Regulation* 8:1.

Hirshhorn, R. 1992. The effects of U.S. Airline Deregulation: A Review of the Literature. In Royal Commission on National Transportation, *Final Report* vol. 4.

Hopkins, T.D. 1992. Cost of Federal Regulation. In T.D. Hopkins, ed. *Regulatory Policy in Canada and the United States*. Proceedings of a Conference. New York: Rochester Institute of Technology.

Jorgenson, D.W. and P.J. Wilcoxen. 1990. Environmental Regulation and U.S. Economic Growth. *Rand Journal of Economics* 21:2.

Khemani, R. 1985. Extent and Evolution of Competition in the Canadian Economy. In D.G. McFetridge, ed. *Canadian Industry in Transition.* Research Studies for the Royal Commission on the Economic Union and Development Prospects for Canada, vol. 2. Toronto: University of Toronto Press.

Lanoie, P. 1989. The Impact of Occupational Health and Safety Regulation on the Incidence of Workplace Accidents: Quebec, 1982-87. Working Paper No. 4189, CRDE, Université de Montréal.

McFetridge, D.G. and A. Lall. 1991. Is There a Theory of Deregulation? In Block and Lermer, eds. *Breaking the Shackles: Deregulating Canadian Industry.* Vancouver: The Fraser Institute.

Mendeloff, J. 1979. *Regulating Safety: An Economic and Political Analysis of Occupational Safety and Health Policy.* Cambridge, MA: MIT Press.

Morrall, J.F. III. 1991. Controlling Regulatory Costs: The Use of Regulatory Budgeting. Paper prepared for meetings of the OECD, Paris, 12-14 November.

National Transportation Agency. 1991. *Annual Review.* Ottawa: Supply and Services Canada.

Noll, R. 1989. Discussion of Peltzman paper. *Brookings Papers on Economic Activity: Microeconomics.* Washington, DC: Brookings Institution.

Peltzman, S. 1976. Toward a More General Theory of Regulation. *Journal of Law and Economics* 19.

_____. 1989. The Economic Theory of Regulation after a Decade of Deregulation. *Brookings Papers on Economic Activity: Microeconomics.* Washington, DC: Brookings Institution.

Pezzey, J. 1992. The Symmetry Between Controlling Pollution by Price and Controlling it by Quantity. *Canadian Journal of Economics* 25:4.

Rea, S.A., Jr. 1983. Regulating Occupational Health and Safety. In D. Dewees, ed. *The Regulation of Quality.* Toronto: Butterworths.

Royal Commission on National Passenger Transportation. 1992. *Final Report.* Ottawa: Supply and Services Canada.

Sherman, L. 1992. Long Distance Competition In Canada Today. Notes for an address at the Angus Telemanagement Group's Conference, Toronto, 11 August.

Stigler, G. 1971. The Theory of Economic Regulation. *Bell Journal of Economics and Management Science* 2.

U.S. Office of Management and Budget. 1992. *Regulatory Program of the U.S. Government.* Washington, DC: OMB.

Van Kooten, G.C. and J. Spriggs. 1984. A Comparative Static Analysis of the Welfare Impacts of Supply Restricting Marketing Boards. *Canadian Journal of Agricultural Economics* 32.

Veeman, M.M. 1987. Marketing Boards: the Canadian Experience. *American Journal of Agricultural Economics,* Proceedings, 69.

Viscusi, W.K. 1986. The Impact of Occupational Safety and Health Regulation, 1973-1983. *Rand Journal of Economics* 17:4.

Williamson, O. 1976. Franchise Bidding for Natural Monopolies: In general and with respect to CATV. *Bell Journal of Economics and Management Science* 7.

Wilson, G.W. 1992. U.S. Passenger Transportation Policy, 1930-1991: An Interpretive Essay. In Royal Commission on National Passenger Transportation, *Final Report* vol. 3.

Zafiriou, B. 1992. Inquiry into Regulation and Competitiveness: Summary of Evidence Received. Prepared for the House of Commons Standing Committee on Finance (sub-committee on regulations and competitiveness), 9 July.

Competitiveness and Regulation

Summary and Comments on
Papers Presented at the Seminar*

*Unabridged papers are in process of publication by the Government and Competitiveness Project.

Regulation of Business Activity

Summary
by *Marcel Boyer*

This study has three basic objectives: (i) to review the fundamental features of the current system of economic regulation in Canada; (ii) to present an overview of the main theoretical advances in the economics of regulation over the past decade; and (iii) to draw conclusions and develop recommendations aimed at improving the efficiency of Canada's regulatory mechanisms in the light of growing globalization of world markets.

The current push for trade liberalization and privatization and the rush to a market economy in certain countries are two sides of the same coin. At the root of these trends is a growing realization that one of the main problems involved in organizing human and social activity in general, and economic activity in particular, is that of providing a proper incentive framework. The efficiency and prosperity of a given economy — defined as a collection of resources (labour, equipment, and natural resources) plus a collection of institutions (government, social, economic, etc.) — will depend not only on the quantity of its available resources, but also (perhaps principally) on the ability and efficiency (i.e., quality) of these institutions to coordinate the various activities (decisions, production, investment, trade, etc.) in order to maximize the potential value of resources and to motivate economic agents to achieve this potential. These institutions include both the firms being regulated and the regulatory mechanisms governing them.

The relationship between a regulatory agency and the firms it regulates is in some ways similar to that between the senior management of a firm (or any organization) and its internal departments, or to that between an employer and his employees. In all three cases, the "principal" (regulatory agency, management, employer) requires his "agent" (regulated firm, department, employee) to behave appropriately within the organization, i.e., by making the maximum contribution to the organization's common objectives (maximizing the welfare of customers, maximizing profits). To this end, the principal must be able to coordinate the agent's activities with the activities of the other members of the organization and to motivate the agent to take, on his own initiative and on the basis of available proprietary information, those courses of action most likely to achieve the organization's objectives. By viewing the regulatory agency and the firm or firms it regulates as members of a single organization with clearly defined objectives, we can draw some interesting and revealing analogies between the regulation of business activity and the operating principles of organizations, particularly when an organization is faced with internal information that is incomplete and asymmetrical.

Recent theoretical developments in economic regulation proceed from the assumption that the central problem of regulation is the organizational inefficiency costs created by inadequate attention to incentive problems relative to pricing problems. Accordingly, information asymmetry must be explicitly modelled, and any assessment of proposed regulatory mechanisms and procedures must take into account the additional constraints that information asymmetry imposes on the task of defining and determining the efficient allocation of resources, i.e., participation and incentive constraints. Participation constraints correspond more or less to the constraints associated with securing adequate financing for regulated activities and adequate returns for investment capital relative to opportunity costs. Incentive constraints reflect the problems associated with adverse selection and moral hazards, phenomena that are omnipresent in economic regulation. Lastly, the constraints associated with public funding of regulated activities are also explicitly modelled in order to examine the underlying reasons for basing price regulation on average costs (i.e., excluding government subsidies) rather than on marginal costs (e.g., including government subsidies to some extent, or as determined by the Ramsey-Boiteux formula under budget equilibrium).

Globalization and the opening of markets to international competition forces firms (like all organizations) to adjust and to face the prospect of greater competition in the years ahead. In addition, the increasingly severe restrictions imposed by international agreements on governments' ability to subsidize certain industries mean that firms must meet the challenge of greater competition without government support. Any delay in implementing policies to promote firms' adjustment and flexibility is likely to have adverse medium-term consequences. Maintaining a regulation system that inhibits competition and allows a degree of laxness or organizational inefficiency to persist in regulated firms will work against the best interests of these firms in the medium run. That is why it is so urgent to overhaul our entire approach to regulated industries and firms.

Governments can make their actions more effective by realizing that implementing a system of incentive regulation and/or deregulation (as appropriate) is a social project, in the sense that it must be coupled with an extensive information and training program aimed at those people, firms and workers most likely to be affected by the current tendency to increase competition and reduce government "protection." In addition to the political problems (pressure groups) that may arise as a result of declines in prices and nominal wages (or even in real or relative wages) in industries formerly subject to extensive regulation, pressures to slow down the reorganization of the structure of these industries may also emerge in response to more flexible entry conditions, declining profits, the inevitable bankruptcies, the emergence of new leaders and possibly the appearance of new forms of industrial concentration at the national level which, without stronger and broader international competition could prove harmful to the economy.

The study leads to a series of recommendations.

Recommendation No. 1: Opt for deregulation first.

In all cases where deregulation is possible because of technological change or changes in national and international competition patterns, governments should introduce deregulation programs that (a) allow firms to adapt to new economic conditions and (b) encourage the entry of new firms into the industries involved.

Recommendation No. 2: Opt for price-cap regulation with "yardstick" competition in a situation of complete information.

When deregulation is not possible or is inadvisable in a situation of complete (but possibly imperfect) information, "fixed-price contract" or "price-cap" regulation should be implemented, whereby prices are determined according to a "common" estimate of either the firm's costs or competitive price levels. Price-cap regulation is particularly appropriate in situations where it replaces regulation based on rates of return or on average-cost pricing. Ideally, price caps should be set according to some kind of yardstick competition at the international or provincial level, as appropriate.

Recommendation No. 3: Opt for incentive regulation with yardstick competition in situations of incomplete information when information rents are unacceptable.

When deregulation is not possible or is inadvisable in a situation of incomplete information where the social cost of information rents is high, incentive regulatory mechanisms should be implemented, whereby firms are offered a choice from among several contracts, each one specifying that any excess profits over the initial target are to be shared in the form of future price cuts or direct reimbursements, and that any shortfall in profits relative to the initial target is to be partially reimbursed in the form of future price increases or direct reimbursement to the firm. This type of regulatory mechanism works best when the percentage of excess profit or shortfall is low and has been determined relative to competitive yardsticks.

Recommendation No. 4: Opt for "Loeb-Magat" style regulation in situations of incomplete information when information rents are acceptable.

When deregulation is not possible or is inadvisable in a situation of incomplete information when the social cost of information rents is low or nil, Loeb-Magat style regulation mechanisms should be put in place. The regulatory agency must determine the demand characteristics of consumers (possibly in conjunction with the firm involved) and make transfers to the firm in proportion to consumer surplus.

Recommendation No. 5: Set up an effective agency that is independent of both governments and regulated firms. Its responsibilities should include:

- reviewing the regulatory system;
- assessing the impact of the system;
- establishing transitional mechanisms and market mechanisms to replace direct regulation; and
- designing public information programs.

The implementation of a system of either incentive regulation and/or deregulation is likely to disrupt, at least momentarily, local products and services in several industries: transportation, telecommunications, education, health care, etc. It is therefore urgent to delegate responsibility for assessing impacts and to identify or establish institutions to determine the most appropriate transitional mechanisms for moving from a protected to an accountable society and for encouraging the adoption of incentive regulation and/or deregulation programs.

In order to help the public accept the gradual elimination of cross-subsidization programs, cross subsidies should be replaced as soon as possible by explicit (tax-based?) subsidies paid directly to consumers in the case of products considered to be socially essential goods. If appropriate, it would also be a good idea to apply a price-cap formula, whereby subsidy amounts would decrease steadily over time according to a pre-determined schedule in order to encourage both adjustment in consumption patterns and the emergence of firms able to produce these products and services more efficiently.

When the primary purpose of regulation is to manage supply in markets subject to significant price variation, it would make sense to encourage the development of futures markets, so that the firms involved will have a means to hedge against excessive price and income fluctuations. Futures markets would also reduce the political pressure for government intervention and could significantly increase markets' efficiency.

It would also be advisable to set up a council, independent of both the regulatory agencies and the regulated firms, with a mandate to review the regulatory system. This should favour a speedy process of ordered rationalization rather than ad hoc responses to the crises that are inevitably generated by the systematic adjustment lags associated with market globalization. This definitely represents a social project.

Comments
by *Christopher Green*

When I was invited to comment on Marcel Boyer's paper I could not know that it would be my last opportunity to participate in a program organized by the Economic Council of Canada. The federal government's unwise decision to "privatize" all independent economic research in Canada is not only a nostalgic reminder of past collaborations (in particular with Jean-Michel Cousineau), but of the many useful research projects carried out by the Economic Council over the past quarter-century. I shall have more to say about "privatization" in my comments.

The paper is an elegant review and analysis of the recent theoretical literature on regulation of firms in traditionally regulated industries. The paper bears the strong imprint of Professor Boyer's superb ability to grasp the analytical heart of a problem: in the present case it is one where (decreasing) cost conditions, demand for non-storable services without close substitutes, principal-agent incentive problems, asymmetric information, and uncertainty conspire to make a conscientious regulator's task a veritable nightmare, while at the same time casting doubt on whether completely unfettered markets, free of any public control, could do better. One also admires Marcel Boyer's policy menu: deregulation where possible, heavier reliance on "price caps" where deregulation is not possible, and more attention to the use of competitive "yardsticks." Small missteps, such as Boyer's recommendation that in certain situations regulators should apply Loeb-Magat (1979) -type regulation, rather than confining it to the classroom where it belongs, do not mar what is otherwise a very useful paper.

In the time allotted to me, I want to expand upon two topics discussed by Professor Boyer: (i) price-cap regulation and (ii) "yardstick competition." I shall conclude with a few provocative comments about the relevance of "optimal regulation."

Price-Cap Regulation

The interest in price cap regulation (PCR) is a healthy development. It is simpler than the more traditional rate-of-return regulation (RORR) and contains more explicit incentives for cost efficiency. The difficulties in choosing the appropriate price index and value of the *X* factor should not disturb regulators. The choice should be viewed as an exercise in experimentation, with rapid changes possible where necessary, as long as the process can avoid most of the adversarial characteristics that tend to plague the operation of RORR.

However, we should not assume that PCR will yield far more efficient performance than does RORR, especially if inflation is kept under control. The reason is that the actual (as opposed to textbook) operation of RORR in non-inflationary periods has much in common with PCR. Almost 20 years ago, Joskow (1974) drew attention to the stark difference between regulation in the world of Averch and Johnson (1962) and regulation in the real world. Citing extensive evidence on the number of formal rate reviews by U.S. regulatory Commissions, Joskow (1974, p. 298) concluded that:

> it *does not* appear that regulatory agencies have been concerned with regulating rates of return per se. The primary concern of regulatory commissions has been to keep *nominal prices from increasing*. Firms which can increase their earned rates of return without raising prices or by lowering prices (depending on changing cost and demand characteristics) have been permitted to earn virtually any rate of return they can. *Formal regulatory action in the form of rate of return review is primarily* triggered *by firms attempting to raise the level of their rates or to make major changes in the structure of their rates*, [emphasis is original]. [National Energy Board regulation of Canadian pipelines could be described in similar terms. C.G.]

This sounds to me a lot like the operation of PCR, except that the latter increases the pressure for cost reduction by including the X factor. But the profit incentives to reduce costs clearly exist in "real world" RORR. Moreover, it is hard to believe that for very capital-intensive enterprises the pressures for increased efficiency would be greater under deregulation than under PCR or "real world" RORR. As long as inflation is more modest than is the scope for cost reduction from scale economies and productivity increases, RORR creates few constraints on, or disincentives to, efficient performance. The one real constraint is the scope for experimentation with *rate structures* although, as Bonbright (1961) makes clear, formal rate reviews usually gave substantial latitude to the regulated firm in choosing a schedule of "non-discriminatory" rates (which would preclude many Ramsey-Boiteux prices) that is consistent with the allowed rate of return.

When inflation struck in the late 1960s and 1970s, the rate of return regulation broke down. The cumbersomeness of RORR proceedings precluded the frequent reviews called for by rapidly rising prices and interest rates. A degree of automaticity was invoked in the form of fuel adjustment clauses. However, inflation brought home the real administrative inefficiency of RORR, even as "regulatory lag" cast doubts on even the theoretical generality of the A-J effect or the extent to which a utility's management could be intentionally x inefficient or otherwise lax in keeping costs under whatever control is possible. Although inflation was finally brought under control in the 1980s, memories of the regulatory havoc it had wrought made the simplicity of PCR attractive. Moreover, because the incentives for efficiency are more explicit in PCR than in RORR, the former is an easier regulatory mode to justify when deregulation is the goal, but is not fully feasible or desirable.

It is important to recognize, however, that under general inflationary conditions PCR will take on most of the cost-plus characteristics of RORR. Once rates of inflation push the rate of change of the price index (PI) to several times the level of the productivity factor, X, the latter becomes of relatively little consequence. Utilities will concentrate on convincing regulators to choose price indexes that adequately reflect the increases in costs that they incur. Except for the length of hearings, PCR will operate much like RORR. If this statement seems doubtful keep in mind that constitutionally (at least in the United States) regulation cannot expropriate the used and useful capital of regulated enterprises (Munn v. Illinois 1877; Smyth v. Ames 1898). It is also interesting that Schmalensee (1989, p. 434-435) found that PCR is superior to RORR only when there is little uncertainty; that "very high levels of uncertainty may make cost-plus regulation superior to any linear scheme that provides incentives for cost reduction." Uncertainty about the future is likely to rise with the rate of inflation.

Yardstick Competition

Towards the end of his paper, Boyer makes reference to the concept of "yardstick competition" (*concurrence balisée*). He does so in the context of choosing a value for the X, or productivity factor, in the price-cap formula. However, the concept of "yardstick competition" is also important in assessing the role of public enterprise in deregulated industries.

In his relatively brief discussion of the deregulation of transportation in Canada, Boyer makes no reference to the role played by public enterprise. Yet one of Canada's most important "experiments" (a distant second only to building a nation on two founding languages and cultures) was its innovative use of public enterprise in competition with private enterprise in sectors regarded as "affected with the public interest." In several industries (airlines, railroads, broadcasting, energy development), Canada sought a middle path between U.S. reliance on heavily regulated private enterprise and Europe's reliance on nationalized industry. The success of this experiment is indicated in two papers by Caves and Christensen (1980, 1981), which compared the performance of U.S. and Canadian railroads and the relative performance of CN and CP before and after effective deregulation in the 1960s. They found that deregulated transportation firms, whether publicly or privately owned, perform much better than privately owned but regulated ones and that public and private firms had comparably efficient performance after deregulation; these findings were totally ignored when Canada came to deregulate the airlines in the 1980s.

It is not surprising that the Canadian government, intellectually committed to deregulation and ideologically committed to privatization, would fail to distinguish the Canadian institutional context from that of the United States (where only deregulation mattered) and the U.K. (where only privatization of nationalized industry really mattered). However, many members of my own profession also appear to have fallen into the trap of assuming that public enterprise is necessarily more interventionist than is regulation. The Economic Council of Canada's otherwise highly informative report, *Minding the Public's Business* (1986), which received input from many academic economists, failed to deal seriously with the findings and implications of Caves and Christensen. Unfortunately, the Economic Council will not be around to do a report card on its own recommendation to privatize Air Canada (among others).

Boyer gives a great deal of attention in his paper to the information requirements of regulation and the difficulties created by asymmetric information. It is perhaps somewhat curious, then, that he did not consider the information content of alternative forms of government intervention — in those cases where conditions may necessitate some role for public involvement. One advantage of competitive public enterprise is that it reduces the extent and importance of asymmetric information by providing government with a "window on the industry." Moreover, I would argue that regulation is a far blunter tool than is competitive private enterprise, where the industry is otherwise free of price, output and entry regulation. Of course, this is *not* an argument for extensive public enterprise. On the contrary, much of the privatization carried out by federal and provincial governments in Canada in the last decade is fully justified. What I am arguing is that deregulation does *not* imply privatization, and that if some form of public control is needed a public enterprise competitor involves less intervention in markets than does regulation of privately-owned firms.

Conclusion

I will conclude with a few parting thoughts — or shots. It is a conceit of economists to believe that what our models tell us matters a great deal. Actually, that conceit might not be so undeserved if our models were less reliant on the optimization framework and calculus that currently is the distinguishing feature of most economic research and publication. The simple fact is, however, that the world will not conform to the one on which our models are implicitly based. In a world where most relevant information is "time and place specific" rather than "scientific" (Hayek 1945), it makes little sense to prescribe formulas requiring large amounts of "scientific" information (such as known demand curves) for the achievement of "optimal regulation." Thus the Loeb-Magat (1979) proposal, to induce marginal-cost pricing by providing the regulated firm with a subsidy equal to consumer surplus, is a non-starter, even if the subsequent application of lump-sum taxes somehow makes the device politically acceptable.

Designing regulatory schemes as if demand and cost conditions are generally known or are similar across enterprises makes little sense to me. If demand and cost conditions make some form of regulation necessary, then the best we can do in a world of Hayekian information is to "satisfice." What is needed are simple, easily understood and accepted rules which are broadly consistent with the growth of economic surplus. Then the gains can be divided between producers and consumers. Everyone will go home happy, even if some economist can show that on his or her assumptions, we could have done better.

Is there a moral to this story? Perhaps. It is hard to imagine that Canada's excellent transportation, telecommunications and energy networks, and the services they provide, are really suffering from current levels of regulation or public ownership. While further privatization, deregulation, or the introduction of incentive regulation may (or may not) be justified, it is hard for me to believe that they are answers to Canada's competitiveness problem.

References

Averch, H. and L. Johnson. 1962. Behaviour of the Firm under Regulatory Constraint. *American Economic Review* 52 (December).

Bonbright, J.C. 1961. *Principles of Public Utility Rates.* New York: Columbia University Press.

Caves, D. and L. Christensen. 1980. The Relative Efficiency of Public v. Private Firms in a Competitive Environment. *Journal of Political Economy* 88 (Sept.-Oct.): 958-976.

_____. 1981. Economic Performance in Regulated and Unregulated Environments: A Comparison of U.S. and Canadian Railroads. *Quarterly Journal of Economics* (November):559-581.

Economic Council of Canada. 1986. *Minding the Public's Business.* Ottawa: Supply and Services Canada.

Hayek, F. 1945. The Use of Knowledge in Society. *American Economic Review* (September): 519-530.

Joskow, P. 1974. Inflation and Environmental Concern: Structural Change in the Process of Public Utility Price Regulation. *The Journal of Law and Economics* (October): 399-404.

Loeb, M. and W.A. Magat. 1979. A Decentralized Method for Utility Regulation. *The Journal of Law and Economics* 20 (Autumn): 399-404.

Schmalensee, R. 1989. Good Regulatory Regimes. *Rand Journal of Economics* 20 (Autumn): 417-436.

Efficient Instruments for Labour Market Regulation

Summary
by *Morley Gunderson*

The Canadian labour market is increasingly affected by labour market policies with a high regulatory component, especially regulations that involve substantial real resource costs to administer, implement and enforce. This regulatory component tends to downplay the market or collective bargaining as alternative mechanisms to achieve the same ends, and to de-emphasize the role of private incentive structures in achieving those ends, and perhaps "undoing" the regulatory intent.

The growing regulatory component is illustrated with respect to a wide variety of labour market policies: pay and employment equity legislation; workers' compensation; hours of work and overtime regulations; wage controls; interest arbitration criteria for wage setting in the public sector; reasonable accommodation requirements; wage extension by judicial decree; pension regulations; and legislative bans on mandatory retirement.

The regulatory aspect is under increased scrutiny in part because of its potential adverse effect on competitiveness. This is an increasingly important consideration given that the competitiveness of our labour market on an international basis is being jeopardized by other factors — strikes, a weak commitment to training, few innovative workplace practices, passive labour market policies that emphasize income maintenance rather than retraining, and increasing unit labour costs (wages adjusted for productivity and the exchange rate), especially relative to our major trading partner, the United States.

The regulatory costs are also under increased scrutiny because the increased mobility of capital investment and plant location decisions mean that firms can move to jurisdictions that do not impose such high regulatory costs, unless the regulations serve an efficiency rationale.

While there are these pressures for regulatory reform, in the labour market as in other markets, there are other pressures to increase the amount of labour market regulation. These pressures emanate from both the demand side of the labour market (industrial restructuring, technological change, mergers and acquisitions, plant closings, bankruptcies, mass layoffs, and the use of contingent workforces) as well as the supply side (aging workforce, increased labour force participation of women, greater ethnic diversity and the dominance of the two-earner family). As well, governments may have an incentive to reduce their budgets by shifting "responsibilities" from public budgets to private employers through regulatory requirements. Dissatisfaction from both labour and management with the conventional legal structure governing labour relations is also increasing pressure for alternative models for regulating the employment relationship.

After reviewing the alternative rationales for labour market regulation, the elements of efficient labour market regulation are discussed and illustrated with respect to a number of Canadian policies. Elements of efficient labour market regulation include: utilizing the mechanisms of the market and collective bargaining; correcting for well-defined market failures and imperfections including the lack of private incentives to train and to innovate with respect to workplace practices; paying attention to the incentive structures of the various stakeholders, including their incentive to utilize the regulatory process for their own ends; building in checks on rent seeking; utilizing adjustment assistance to encourage rather than discourage change in the direction of market forces; paying attention to efficiency in achieving legitimate distributional objectives and in the design, implementation, administration and enforcement of regulations; focusing on the real resource costs of the regulations; involving stakeholders in the design, implementation and administration of the regulations; and having well-defined responsibility among the various participants — labour and management, different administrative agencies, and different labour jurisdictions.

Utilizing such elements of efficient labour market regulation, and integrating them with the mechanisms of the market and collective bargaining where appropriate, will help achieve the legitimate objectives of such regulations in a manner that is consistent with both competitiveness and fairness.

Comments
by *Jean-Michel Cousineau*

The aim of Professor Gunderson in this study was to develop some guiding principles for government decisions regarding the regulation of Canadian labour markets. The approach was as follows: first, analyze the factors affecting the demand for labour market regulation, the various supply constraints, the arguments in favour of such intervention and the (implicit) arguments against it, and then examine how these factors are manifested on the Canadian labour market.

Generally speaking, the conclusions of the paper may be summed up in terms of three broad guidelines:

First, before even starting to define and implement new regulatory mechanisms, it is essential to ensure that (a) there really is a problem that labour markets are unable to solve and (b) the measure is not simply an attempt to satisfy the special interests of a particular pressure group to the detriment of the public or collective interest.

Second, assuming that regulation is indeed warranted, it is essential to ensure that the problem is clearly circumscribed, that the regulatory action directly targets that problem, and that market and incentive mechanisms are given as large a role as possible.

Third, the chosen method of regulation must be consistent with all recognized criteria of management efficiency (e.g., achievement of objectives at least cost) and the demands that this type of intervention will make on the real resources of the economy must be carefully considered.

The comments that I would like to offer on this study will focus on three points: (i) the particular characteristics of the labour market, (ii) the historical context, and (iii) empirical documentation.

The Particular Characteristics of the Labour Market

In my view, what is particular about labour markets in terms of regulation is the central place occupied by problems related to equity and income redistribution, such as the problems of pay equity, employment equity, and fair treatment for the disabled. A product in the goods and services market cares little whether its price is lower than that of another product that is technically of equal value, or whether it is being discriminated against. However, human beings are not so tolerant of such treatment. One of the driving forces behind the gradual growth of labour market regulation is what might be termed the "right of recognition" or the "right of human dignity." While this factor has been explicitly recognized by historians and philosophers (e.g., Fukuyama 1992), to my knowledge it has not been included per se in economic analyses of welfare. I cannot help but wonder whether this type of concept might prove better suited than the more traditional concepts of equity and income distribution to describing this new form of regulation. In any event, I feel that it is well worth trying to determine what is specific to the labour market and what is not as part of our attempts to understand certain phenomena that are likely to grow in importance in the years ahead. I might add in this regard that the most common feature of labour market regulation is the desire to protect the most disadvantaged or weakest members of society (although the results vary in efficiency and may be partially offset by other groups[1]). This obviously poses a problem for condition (b) of the first guideline, unless increasing the welfare of the interest groups involved will contribute to the welfare of better-off members of society as well, through altruism. In short, it may be that what distinguishes the new regulation of labour markets from other types of regulation is the incorporation of the human factor and the quest for recognition and dignity.

The Historical Context

Historically speaking, regulation of or on labour markets dates back to their first appearance in the early days of the industrial revolution. A maximum work day of 10 hours was first instituted for women and children in the late nineteenth century, followed by minimum wages for women in the early twentieth. The major provisions of workplace health and safety regulation were also among the earliest forms of labour market regulation.[2] These measures essentially concern fundamental rights related to the protection of the physical and moral integrity of human beings. In fact, I am tempted to suggest that, historically, regulation has represented the initial response to a change in the environment, later to be replaced by more complex, more elaborate and (ideally) more efficient formulas on a more permanent basis. This has been true of workplace health and safety (and may also be the case for the current reaction to environmental problems).

Today — and historically this is quite a recent trend — governments in Canada have largely abandoned their traditional methods for regulating workplace health and safety in favour of more decentralized approaches that leave it to joint business committees to determine by and for themselves what regulatory mechanisms are needed to ensure adequate investment in safety.

Let me cite one last example to flesh out this theory. The minimum wage which, as noted above, was one of the earliest forms of labour market regulation, has declined considerably in relative terms over the past 20 years in Canada. In 1970, the minimum wage was 51 percent of the average industrial wage in this country. By 1988, it was only 35 percent. That represents a drop of 16 percentage points or 31 percent (Seccareccia 1991). It would thus appear that regulation is essentially an instinctive reaction that declines into irrelevance and inefficiency after a certain period of time, eventually to be replaced by more sophisticated systems of management and later by other forms of regulation that are themselves responses to different sets of needs.

Empirical Documentation

Finally, I consider it regrettable that Gunderson's study was unable to document the growth of regulation in Canada. The paper notes simply that the precise documentation on the growing regulatory component of labour market policies was not carried out. Obviously, this makes it hard to place this development in the proper temporal context. No dates are given for the adoption of the various regulatory mechanisms. We are not sure whether we are speaking of the 1950s, sixties, seventies or 1980s. Nor do we know the extent and scope of the changes involved. In the case of limits on hours of work, for instance, we are not told when the changes took place and how extensive they were. In the case of pay equity, I do know that such policies emerged first and foremost in Manitoba for the public sector and that they have given rise to some extensive adjustments (in the neighbourhood of $3,000 to $4,000, as noted in Gunderson's text). I also know that in January 1990 Ontario adopted a fairly radical program aimed at both private and public enterprise. In Quebec, on the other hand, I know that pressures are building in favour of employment equity and pay equity measures, but that the Quebec government, in accordance with its current wage policy, refuses to consider the problem from this angle, preferring instead to speak of relative wages without reference to sex.

To fully argue the hypothesis of growing labour market regulation, therefore, I feel that a more detailed survey of the issue in both quantitative and qualitative terms is required.

Conclusion

My purpose in making these comments is simply to point out that documentation is required in order, first, to authoritatively state that labour market regulation has been growing in Canada; second, to identify the specific factors affecting labour market regulation, which also serve to distinguish it from regulation in other markets; and, third, to place labour market regulation in a historical perspective or context that highlights the qualitative changes that must be considered when arguing that it is growing or following an upward trend.

To conclude, I consider Professor Gunderson's paper to be a pioneering work in terms of the quality of the analysis and its recommendations. These recommendations should prove very useful to the task of developing principles to guide labour market regulation decisions in Canada.

Notes

1. See Jean-Luc Migué, "Le salaire minimum ou quand le diable se fait moine," on these issues, particularly minimum wage policies.

2. It could be argued that regulation was more extensive in the early part of this century. One need only consider the body of regulation that underpinned the development of our modern, highly complex liberal economies. Pension fund regulation, which Professor Gunderson mentions in her paper, might well be considered an example of this type of regulation (e.g., governing fraud, embezzlement, and other breaches of trust).

References

Fukuyama, Francis. 1992. *The End of History and the Last Man*. Toronto: Macmillan.

Migué, Jean-Luc. 1977. Le salaire minimum ou quand le diable se fait moine. *Relations industrielles/Industrial Relations* 32, 3: 310-319.

Seccareccia, Mario. 1991. Salaire minimum, emploi et productivité dans une perspective post-keynésienne. *Actualité économique* 67, 2: 166-191.

Social Efficiency: Models of Efficiency Wages, Fair Wages and Competitiveness

Summary
by *Ronald Wintrobe* and *Robert Young*

Précis

Competitiveness depends in the end on the productive efficiency of a national economy. This paper broadens out standard neo-classical notions of efficiency to present a new focus on "social efficiency." It does so by exploring new models of "efficiency wages" and of "fair wages." Beyond this, we draw some policy implications of these models and of their combination into a model of social efficiency.

Executive Summary

In economics, the standard recipe for competitiveness pre-scribes free trade, non-inflationary monetary policy, and minimal government intervention in the private sector. This recipe has several flaws. First, it is based on a one-sector model of the economy in which all markets clear and in which the internal organization and management of firms is entirely neglected. Second, empirically, in the most successful economies over the past three decades (Japan, Germany, Korea) one finds a substan-tial government presence in the economy, along with firm and sectoral organizational and management structures which are unusual and innovative by North American standards. Last, the operation of unfettered markets provides little economic security. Yet people want security, and in democracies they will vote and organize for policies that provide it. In the standard neo-classical approach, the resulting political interventions such as rent controls, tariffs, and minimum wages are decried as inefficient, but they are the natural result of the failure of economic markets to provide people with something they want.

Recent economic models of "efficiency wages" and "fair wages" provide the basis for an alternative approach to competitiveness.

Efficiency wage models focus on the internal organization of firms, especially the "effort elicitation problem"; that is, how employees can be motivated to work hard and to make decisions that further the interest of the organization. The point of departure of this work is that the firm has to be able to detect and punish — or to minimize — "shirking" by the employees. However, if labour markets clear, this is impossible, simply because market clearing implies that a worker who is fired can always get another job at the going wage. So, either markets do not clear (and unemployment is a necessary feature of modern economies), or there exists a secondary sector, characterized by "bad jobs" where monitoring workers is relatively easy. Empirical work shows that both features — persistent unemployment and dual labour markets — are characteristic of the Canadian economy. Indeed, since the late 1960s, the Canadian labour market increasingly has become polarized into two sectors. One has "good jobs," with high wages, job security, and good promotion possibilities; the other has jobs with none of these attributes.

In the light of efficiency wage models of such economies, competitiveness is increased by generating more good jobs. Countries with superior management structures and with sound industrial policies which protect and subsidize the high-wage sector will end up with relatively more good jobs, and other countries will tend to have the bad jobs.

A central feature of efficiency wage models is that productive efficiency rests upon the gap between good-sector and bad-sector wages. This also is its central flaw, because it implies that wage gaps will exist between otherwise equal individuals. And this leads to the second pillar of competitiveness.

In a two-sector model, the distribution of economic rewards will be perceived as unfair, and this perception has economic, social and political consequences which themselves reduce competitive-

ness. For example, workers who perceive themselves to be ex-
cluded from the good jobs in the primary sector may turn to
sabotage, or to individual or social pathologies (crime, drugs,
domestic abuse and so on), or they may become a burden on the
tax-transfer system by taking short-term jobs to qualify for unemployment insurance or by going on welfare. The larger the wage
gap between the two sectors, the more severe these consequences
will be.

Moreover, since unemployment exists and bad jobs provide no
security, workers will demand that this be provided by governments. In this they are joined by workers with good jobs in
declining sectors, who are afraid of being displaced into the
secondary sector. Hence, the polarization of the economy into
high- and low-wage sectors creates economic losses directly
through crime and alienation and also through political responses to the rent-seeking, which is stimulated by the unfair-
ness of the system. Social efficiency is the point at which these
losses are balanced by the economic gains that result, according
to the efficiency-wage model, from the wage gap.

Several sets of policy implications can be drawn from this pair
of models of the two-sector economy. First, the efficiency-wage
model suggests that policies that promote the creation of good
jobs may increase national competitiveness. These include subsidies for research and development, favourable procurement
policies, and limited protection. As well, there is a strong case for
subsidizing experimentation with alternative management structures and monitoring systems. Obviously, labour-force training
and retraining must accompany growth in the primary sector.

The fair-wage model poses the problems of how much security
should be provided in the secondary sector and of how to provide
it — through regulating firms, encouraging collective organization, or directly by the state. At least as important is the provision
of opportunities for advancement, because opportunity reduces
frustration and its negative economic consequences. There must
be provision for advancement, both within this sector and from
these bad jobs into the good jobs sector.

Both models focus on human-capital formation. The relationship between this and security-enhancing policies like social

assistance and unemployment insurance suggests that it is desirable to integrate government programs much more tightly than is now the case, and to allow more scope for experimentation and innovation in program design.

Comments
by John O'Grady

The paper that Professor Young and Professor Wintrobe have prepared is highly original and extremely well argued. Young and Wintrobe put the problem of how to elicit employee commitment and effort at the centre of the debate on competitiveness. By doing so, they address important issues in the real world of decision making at the workplace. The script they write has lines for management and for employees. However, there is a third player on the stage. The script must somehow be rewritten to take account of that player. The player to which I am referring is the trade union movement.

"Efficiency wage" theory and its recast version, "fair wage" theory, take no specific cognizance of unions in the employee decision about commitment and effort. This, I believe, is a weakness in the theory. More importantly, it is a weakness that is particularly relevant to those segments of the economy about which the debate over competitiveness is being argued with the greatest vigour.

The manufacturing and resource industries still make up the preponderance of the traded sector. If we set aside the salaried staff in those industries, approximately 70 percent of what we might call "direct production workers" are covered by collective bargaining agreements. There is not, I believe, a manager in any of these industries who believes that the attitude of trade unions is irrelevant to decisions about where to invest. In their study on American industrial relations, Kochan, Katz and McKerskie point to a pattern of disinvestment in unionized plants as an important element in corporate planning. Canadian labour codes do not provide anything comparable to the American sunbelt or to indulgence in employer resistance to unionization. Given the difference in our labour codes, therefore, a decision to avoid unionization is likely to imply a preference for investing outside Canada. While it would be an exaggeration to say that industrial relations factors determine investment decisions, the evidence that they are important cannot be ignored. It would be surreal to script trade unions as mere "extras" on the stage with no lines and no significant part to play.

Both "efficiency wage" theory and its recast version — what Young and Wintrobe refer to as "fair wage" theory — focus on the wage-effort bargain. In addition to the wage-effort bargain, there are, I believe, two other bargains that are important to understanding the economic significance of how the employment relationship is configured. The first of these bargains operates in both the unionized and non-unionized workplaces. It is a bargain over flexibility and security. Paul Osterman has suggested that the wage system and the salary system are fundamentally different bargains about flexibility and security. The salary system is based on a comparatively high degree of employment security and a correspondingly high degree of flexibility in regard to work assignments. By contrast the wage system, especially in the private sector, is characterized by much less employment security and much less employer flexibility in the assignment of work.

There is also a second bargain. It is specific to a unionized workplace. The operative terms in this bargain are the degree of management's recognition of the union as a partner and correspondingly the degree of cooperation extended by the union in the implementation of new technology and new forms of work organization. What prevails in most workplaces is a low trust bargain, that is to say, low levels of recognition in exchange for low levels of cooperation. Indeed, in many workplaces it would be more accurate to say that there is no substantive bargain. Rather, there are competing strategies of union displacement on the one hand and malicious compliance on the other — what Thorstein Veblen referred to as the "conscientious withdrawal of efficiency."

To borrow a phrase from Young and Wintrobe's paper, the current bargains in the traded sector over flexibility and security and over recognition and cooperation are "socially inefficient" bargains. If we do not devise a strategy to achieve a "negotiated adjustment" the prevailing "socially inefficient bargains" will discourage needed investment and impede the growth of productivity. Professor Young and Professor Wintrobe would focus public policy on industrial strategy and human capital formation. While nothing that I have said detracts from their argument, the import of my comments is to attach much greater significance to industrial relations factors and to what is loosely called the "social bargain." Significantly more of this has been occurring in recent years at the sectoral level and at the provincial level than at the national level. My central argument, however, is that in the absence of qualitatively different bargains at the workplace over flexibility and security and over recognition and cooperation, the returns to industrial strategy and to increased investment in human capital formation will disappoint their advocates.

One other short observation that I would make pertains to the effect on the voluntary effort and commitment of workers of their perception of management's plans for the future of their plant. Workers know when management is investing in ongoing modernization and when it is treating a plant as a "cash-cow." As William Lazonick points out "once workers perceive that management ... is taking the managerial surplus out of the enterprise rather than putting it back in and that the firm can no longer offer the employment stability, wage levels and work conditions that it had in the past, cooperative shop-floor relations will turn into conflict."

Select Bibliography

Kochan, Thomas A., Harry C. Katz and Robert B. McKerskie. 1986 and 1989. *The Transformation of American Industrial Relations.* New York: Harper.

Osterman, Paul. 1988. *Employment Futures.* New York: Oxford University Press.

Lazonick, William. 1990. The Basic Analytics of Shop-Floor Value Creation. In *Competitive Advantage on the Shop Floor.* Cambridge, MA: Harvard University Press.

Reducing the Burden of Environmental Regulation

Summary
by *Donald Dewees*

This paper seeks to identify opportunities for improving the cost-effectiveness of environmental regulation in Canada. The focus is on air and water pollution, both conventional and toxic, and regulation at the federal and provincial level. Waste disposal, land contamination, and environmental impact assessment, while important, are considered only peripherally. The investigation includes the regulatory process as well as the regulations themselves. Costs include expenditures by governments and by polluters on the development of regulations, monitoring, compliance and enforcement. Time and delay are recognized as costs along with direct expenditures.

Most pollution damage occurs to parties that are not in a contractual or ongoing relationship with the polluter, thus the market does not force the polluter to internalize the cost that his pollution imposes. Tort law might cause such internalization, by forcing the polluter to compensate victims for the harm that they suffer, but in practice this occurs rarely. Tort doctrine provides primary protection to interests connected with land, but does not protect general ecosystem values or the interest of the general public. More important, most pollution imposes minor harm on a large number of individuals making litigation uneconomical. Perhaps most important, however, we have very limited knowledge of the harm that most pollutants may cause to human health, crop yields, forest growth, terrestrial or aquatic ecosystems, or global climate change. Courts are not, and will not be in the foreseeable future, in a position to evaluate the physical harm caused by most discharges, much less to value them for the purpose of awarding damages. Tort law has not in the past been an effective means of pollution abatement. I am sceptical about expanding tort litigation to control pollution because I do not believe that the current state of scientific knowledge regarding the effects of pollutants would allow courts to play a more predictable and constructive role than they presently do. By default, we must rely on government regulation as the principal means of control.

Governments, too, face the problem of determining the harm caused by pollutants so that reasonable regulations may be adopted. Here again the deficiencies in scientific knowledge raise grave problems. While concern has been expressed regarding hundreds of chemical substances, the number of substances for which harm to human health or to specific plant or animal species has been proven at environmental concentrations is very small. The number of substances for which we have an accurate dose-response function or know of a threshold below which no harm occurs is smaller still. Where evidence exists, it often suggests that over a range of environmental concentrations more is worse and less is better; it is less common to find that there is a "safe threshold" below which there is no harm and above which there is serious harm. This suggests that the goal of environmental policy should usually be to reduce emissions or concentrations of harmful substances until costs become unreasonable, rather than to achieve a specific environmental concentration.

The federal and provincial governments have adopted some ambient air and water quality guidelines that serve as goals for environmental policy. A substantial number of regulations have also been adopted limiting the discharge of substances into the air and the water; additional unenforceable guidelines are also common. Many of these regulations and guidelines limit discharge in relation to process inputs (kg/calorie) or process outputs (kg/kg of product). A smaller number limit the concentration of the substance in the waste stream. Some limit the total mass of discharge of a pollutant from individual plants. Recent regulations often require that emissions not exceed those produced by the "best available technology," sometimes in pursuit of the goal of "virtual elimination" of the discharge of toxic substances. The cost of determining what this means for dozens of substances and thousands of industrial processes is enormous, and the adoption of such regulations has proceeded slowly.

The existing regulatory structure is criticized for imposing costs greater than needed to achieve the desired environmental result, for delaying the construction and expansion of facilities, for failing to regulate strictly, for regulating some substances too strictly while ignoring others, and for adopting regulations too slowly. One set of proposed reforms is the adoption of market mechanisms — the effluent charge and marketable pollution permits. Both are said to reduce the cost of achieving a given level of environmental protection, to speed the regulatory and approval process, to enhance technological progress in pollution control, and to allow more strict control than could otherwise be afforded. Both arouse opposition because they are relatively untried, because it is said to be immoral to sell the environment, because they appear to provide less certainty regarding local environmental quality, because they are not needed if the regulation should allow zero discharge, and because some environmentalists view any markets with suspicion. Other reforms include the use of enforcement incentives, the use of plant "bubbles," regulating more substances less strictly, explicitly considering costs and benefits in setting limits, and the provision of public information regarding substances present and discharged from facilities.

Market policies, both effluent charges and marketable pollution rights, seem likely to improve the cost-effectiveness of environmental regulations and to speed the process of emission reduction for a variety of pollution problems. They might be advantageous in situations where best available technology is the basis for regulation of acid gas emissions, of some toxic emissions, for ozone control, and for controlling global pollutants. Economic enforcement incentives are probably valuable, and their use could probably be expanded. Plant "bubbles" may be of some use, except in cases where current regulations set plant-wide limits. The provision of public information may be valuable in some cases, but it may cause overreaction in others, so it increases uncertainty. It seems likely that increasing the pace at which we regulate substances by imposing less stringent limits on a larger number of substances, at least as an interim measure, would be useful. Finally, where policies set environmental quality goals, we should consider whether the goal represents a concentration at which harm increases sharply or not; if not, then we should be flexible in the pursuit of that goal.

Comments
by *George Kowalski*

Professor Dewees' paper is an excellent exposé of the state-of-play in Canada on the formulation and use of environmental regulations. The paper provides a good discussion of the economic nature of environmental problems, the large range of uncertainty surrounding most environmental issues and particularly the considerable scientific uncertainty in establishing environmental harm. It provides a balanced description of the Canadian Environmental Regulatory Framework and thoughtful suggestions on how to improve the system, and on the desirable direction for future change. The paper's central message is similar to that in *Canada's Green Plan*, the Government of Canada's comprehensive national strategy and action plan for sustainable development. This message is that governments need to regulate "smarter" while at the same time exploring all avenues for new and cost-effective methods of meeting Canada's environmental goals — for example, by using economic instruments.

According to Dewees, we currently have, broadly speaking, very limited knowledge of the harm that most pollutants may cause to human health and to the environment, i.e., it is difficult to establish cause and effect and the dose-response function. This is one of the principal reasons, according to him, that greater reliance on the judicial system (i.e., on liability suits) would not necessarily be a constructive and useful development.

By the same token, however, I would submit that the problem of determining harm makes cost-benefit analysis a rather questionable proposition. If this is the case, how does one square this with the recommendation by the Economic Council, the federal Treasury Board, and others that cost-benefit analysis be applied to regulatory programs in order to enhance overall regulatory efficiency?

It would be useful to have Dewees explore this dilemma in greater depth. What should be the role of cost-benefit analysis in the formulation of environmental regulations? Ought environmental targets and standards be set mainly through political and public debate and negotiations? Should rigorous analytical scrutiny and quantification be applied solely to the methods of achieving the agreed-upon targets? In other words, can the problem be boiled down to assessing and selecting the cost-minimizing solution to achieving a predetermined level of pollution abatement judged desirable by politicians and the public? Compliance costs, after all, are more readily estimated than benefits, even though considerable uncertainties still remain.

Increasingly, environmental issues are being viewed from a sustainable development standpoint. While Dewees recognizes the growing concern about ecosystems, and noted that some environmental issues raise intergenerational considerations, he did not explore the nature of environmental problems within the context of sustainable development. This is receiving more and more attention nowadays.

While it is beyond the scope of Dewees' paper to review in depth all major environmental legislation in Canada, there are a couple of omissions worth highlighting with respect to the *Canadian Environmental Protection Act* (CEPA). At the federal level, this Act is the central guideline for the protection of the environment, and the life and health of Canadians. Since its proclamation in June 1988, 20 regulations have been put in place under the Act. Pursuant to this legislation, the federal government is committed to completing the assessment of 44 potentially hazardous substances. The first substances to be assessed under the Act were dioxins and furans. Proposed regulations for the control of these substances in pulp and paper mill effluents were published in *The Canada Gazette* in December 1991. In total, upwards of 60 new regulations could be introduced under CEPA over the next three years.

To reduce overlap and duplication as well as to promote harmonization, CEPA provides for two mechanisms to facilitate co-operative implementation of national standards: equivalency agreements and administrative agreements. An equivalency agreement suspends the operation of a valid federal regulation in favour of a provincial regulation. Administrative agreements represent a work-sharing partnership for the administration of CEPA. These two provisions are specifically intended to enhance the efficiency of the regulatory process.

Professor Dewees highlights the fact that the formulation of regulations is time consuming and thus can slow down the pace of pollution abatement and cause delays in bringing new plants, processes or products on-line. He further advocates that it may be better for regulatory agencies to avoid setting strict controls on a few substances, but rather concentrate their efforts on regulating many substances even if these controls are not overly stringent in the first instance. This is wise counsel indeed. However, this may be more difficult to do than it would first appear if the intent is to implement enforceable regulations. Obviously, as pointed out by the author, avenues other than regulation can perhaps be pursued to achieve this objective.

Under CEPA, for example, generally the first step in the process of regulation is an assessment of the scientific problem and the release of a report that details the toxicological problem and the scientific basis for control action. If warranted, a strategy options report is then prepared and public consultations undertaken. If the preferred approach is a regulatory one, drafting of regulations follows, involving further consultations as well as the preparation of a Regulatory Impact Analysis Statement (RIAS). (This statement would also include an evaluation of non-regulatory approaches.) Depending on the complexity of the issue, this entire process can take more than three years from inception to final publication of new regulations. It needs to be recognized that the consultation process, particularly when consultations take place at every stage of the development of regulations, takes time.

Historically, environmental regulators in Canada, including Environment Canada, have favoured command-and-control type approaches. More and more, Environment Canada is trying to achieve a better balance between the traditional regulatory approach and newer and more innovative approaches such as voluntary compliance, environmental information, and economic instruments. The department is increasingly supporting the development of environmental codes of practice and guidelines, encouraging the use of environmental audits by companies and government agencies and is at the forefront of federal efforts to provide and disseminate information for changing behaviour in the marketplace.

As well, Environment Canada, in conjunction with the Department of Finance, will soon be releasing a discussion paper on the use of economic instruments. The paper systematically explores the practical issues that must be addressed in selecting and applying specific economic instruments to specific environmental problems facing Canada. Its purpose is to inform stakeholders of key practical considerations and possible options for addressing them. It is also to provide a starting point for the next step, that is, for wide-ranging consultations with Canadians.

Professor Dewees' summary of the arguments for and against the use of emission charges and tradeable permits parallels the information given in our own economic instruments discussion paper. It therefore should come as no surprise that we fully agree with the thrust of his recommendations to move to greater use of market-based instruments. On this subject, it is worth noting that the possibility of using emissions trading to further reduce SO_2 emissions, in addition to reducing NOx/VOc emissions as pointed out in Dewees' paper, is already being explored by a federal-provincial committee under the auspices of the Canadian Council of Ministers of the Environment.

I would now like to close on a more general note. The classic view is that regulations impose costs on the economy and hence are an impediment to competitiveness and growth. Clearly, environmental regulations do impose costs on industry and households. However, the important consideration is whether these are additional costs or simply a transfer (redistribution) of costs from the environment itself, other sectors of the economy and individuals, to polluters. The objective of regulation is to internalize environmental costs while at the same time minimizing the imposition of regulatory process costs. Dewees' paper deals with the issue of minimizing regulatory process costs. I can assure you that this is a high priority for Environment Canada.

On the issue of competitiveness and growth, it is also important to recognize that using environmentally unsound production practices or selling environmentally damaging products is not the basis for a real competitive advantage in an increasingly sophisticated, demanding and environmentally conscious marketplace. A healthy environment and prosperous economy are mutually reinforcing. More than ever, governments, industry and households have to recognize that good environmental policy is good economics. Through *Canada's Green Plan*, the government has sought to engage all Canadians in the pursuit of a healthy environment and prosperous economy flowing from a policy of sustainable development.

A Preliminary Survey of the Impact of Environmental Assessments on Competitiveness

Summary
by *George Neufeld*

Introduction

The objective of this survey was to assemble information on the impact of environmental assessment (EA) processes on competitiveness in Canada. The results will be used as part of a broader initiative being undertaken by the Economic Council of Canada on "Efficient, Smarter Government" at the request of the prime minister.

Environmental assessment (EA) processes are prescribed by federal and provincial government legislation to ensure that the environmental impacts of projects are acceptable prior to the project proceeding to implementation. The processes allow for public input and, if necessary, public hearings. EA processes generally apply to all federal government capital projects as well as private sector capital projects to which federal and/or provincial environmentally related regulations apply.

The findings are based on contacts with about 50 persons, 15 of whom were able to provide extensive information. In-depth telephone interviews were conducted with these 15 persons, most of whom are senior executives in the forestry, pulp and paper, mining, and oil and gas industries. The interviews focused on the costs, factors that contribute to the costs and duration, benefits, key concerns and suggested improvements to EA processes. The information obtained on concerns about EA processes provided the insight required to provide a first-order identification of the impact of EA processes on competitiveness.

Findings

A proponent's cost of EA processes for major projects is as much as 4 percent of a project's total capital cost, but most often much less. Major projects are defined here as projects whose capital costs are at least $3-5 million. In absolute terms, an EA process for a major project costs between a hundred thousand dollars to as much as $5-7 million. The key factor affecting the cost of an EA process appears to be whether or not the project is a completely new development, i.e., the cost of an EA process for a new mine, gas production plant or pulp and paper plant will tend to be higher than for a project to expand a mine, plant or a mill. However, more data would be required to establish a definitive relationship between size and type of project and the EA process costs. The duration of an EA process is generally 1.5 to 2.5 years.

Proponents' main concern about EA processes is not the cost but the uncertainty associated with having to wait until the end of the process to know whether approval will be granted or denied. The proponent must develop detailed plans for the project in order to undertake a complete environmental assessment for the EA process. A proponent's investment may represent millions of dollars and up to 14 percent of the total capital cost of the project by the time that the EA process has been completed. Making these up-front investments without knowing whether approval will be granted is the cause for the proponents' concern. Uncertainty is exacerbated when there are significant delays in completing the EA process, particularly if market or economic conditions change.

Other EA process-related concerns raised by proponents include: (i) the lack of ground rules concerning intervenors; (ii) the multiplicity of government agencies that become involved; (iii) the lack of ground rules concerning government agencies' requests for information; (iv) regulators sometimes being reluctant to approve use of not-yet operationally-proven technology; and (v) the apparent increased future involvement of the federal government with projects that have in the past been solely of provincial interest. These factors contribute to the uncertainties and delays associated with EA processes.

Proponent-suggested improvements to EA processes include:

- Provide proponents with "one window" to deal with government, e.g., a designated agency that would determine and reconcile the requirements of all government agencies;
- Establish a phased approach with approval in principle to be granted or denied at the end of the first phase;
- Establish agreement among all parties at the outset of the EA process on the scope of issues to be addressed, the schedule and ground rules concerning requests from government agencies and demands from intervenors;
- Provide conditional approvals if a proponent proposes to use an approach or technology that has not yet been operationally proven elsewhere.

Industry is reluctant to talk about the broader adverse implications of EA processes in Canada. However, there is increased concern and wariness of EAs among private sector companies and investors as a result of the headlines generated by such projects as the Oldman River Dam, the Rafferty/Alameda Dam and James Bay Hydro Dam as well as the difficulties associated with the Class Environmental Assessment for Timber Management on Crown lands in Ontario, Ontario Hydro's Demand/Supply Plan and the Ontario Waste Management Corporation's Waste Disposal Plan. Interviewees noted that difficulties and frustrations with EAs could result in companies deciding to seek opportunities outside Canada, particularly if there are other factors that discourage investment in Canada.

Conclusion

Notwithstanding the relevant concerns, EA processes do not appear to have an adverse impact on Canada's competitive position in the global economy. However, there are cases where the EA processes have contributed to increasing the capital cost of the project without any apparent reduction in the projects' overall environmental impacts. While proponents of such projects did not suggest that these increased costs were sufficient to make the proposed venture or expansion non-viable or non-competitive, it does not seem prudent to incur unnecessary cost increases in times of stiff competition.

In the past, EA processes do not appear to have been a significant factor in industry deciding to invest or locate outside Canada. However, there are indications that the business community could become wary of future investments in Canada that are subject to an EA process, particularly if the current concerns are not resolved and the federal government becomes more involved with projects that have in the past been solely of provincial concern.

Improving EA processes would have the effect of "nipping the above mentioned problems in the bud." Furthermore, EA processes that are efficient and deal effectively with the critical issues are more likely to hasten the adoption of sustainable development principles than will a process that is frustrating for all concerned. It would appear to be feasible to improve EA processes without jeopardizing environmental objectives.

Recommendation

This survey has produced a useful by-product: several suggestions for improving EA processes. However, in order to engage key stakeholders in dialogue that focuses on if and how EA processes could be improved, it is recommended that this survey be expanded to include direct involvement of key stakeholders to build a consensus on the most urgent concerns that need to be addressed and the manner in which to address them. The outcome should be an action plan and a commitment to proceed to the implementation of agreed upon improvements.

Comments
by *André Marsan*

My comments will be mainly of a general nature, touching upon some related topics with which we are all familiar.

I believe that, today, a well-managed corporation or firm is subject to two different types of accountability. We are all familiar with financial accountability. A corporation is required to report to its shareholders and to prepare financial balance sheets, forecasts and development programs. Should the corporation run into difficulty, reorganization plans will be drawn up and discussed in conjunction with its financial statements.

In 1992, a well-managed corporation must also address the question of environmental accountability. Where it used to report only to its financial shareholders, now it must also report to the public, which is the general shareholder of all corporations. It must prepare an environmental balance sheet and demonstrate that it is complying with existing law and regulations. Should it run into difficulty, plans must be drawn up to correct the situation.

As you know, financial institutions now demand an "environment audit" before lending to corporations. This means that the financial firms themselves require proof of compliance with the two types of accountability. A financial balance sheet alone is no longer enough. In this respect, an environmental assessment is similar to a business plan. No one would dare approach a financial institution without a business plan that includes forecasts, assumptions and future projections regarding the profitability of the firm or the particular project proposed to shareholders.

It goes without saying that the audience for a business plan consists of financial institutions, financial shareholders, government economic departments, and municipal officials. The environmental "business plan" (i.e., the environmental impact study), too, is intended for financial shareholders, because "environmental" and "economic" issues are now inseparable. The plan is also submitted to financial institutions, because they will only be interested in lending to projects that conform to environmental

standards. It is also intended for government economic departments. Quebec's Société de développement industriel is considering attaching an environmental clause to its loans. Lastly, it is
intended for municipal officials, unions, the local population and
the department of the environment, which are all concerned with
environmental issues from their particular perspectives.

I do not think that it is the principle here that is at issue, but
the process. Is it too legalistic, bureaucratic, too long or still
poorly defined? Some would go so far as to say that Quebec's
Bureau d'audiences publiques sur l'environnement operates like
an inquisition. Generally speaking, the process is not consistent
with that normally required by investors. Neither is the process
consistent with the project's timetable or with the objective of
economic development. In Quebec, for example, developing the
guidelines on the content of an environmental impact study takes
at least a year and sometimes up to 18 months. These guidelines
are a mixed bag — more a collection of requests for information
than a well-defined program or study protocol. This may be one
of the most important causes of the problem.

In my opinion, an environmental impact study should be
similar to an economic study. Its main aim should be to gauge
the future environmental costs and benefits associated with a
specific project.

The solution proposed by the federal government is to institute
prior consultation on the guidelines. I fear that this suggestion
— developing a set of guidelines that satisfies all concerned —
would add another 12 months or so to the process. And if the
guidelines remain merely a sort of table of contents, the results
will inevitably be a mass of information of no use to the assessment of future environmental impacts. Requirements such as
these impede creativity and distract attention from the real problems and the main issues.

I believe that what we must do is transfer responsibility to the
firm and its consultant. As you well know, a financial analyst who
delivers a faulty analysis or a chartered accountant who verifies
books that turn out to be incorrect will quickly find himself out
of a job. We should adopt the same attitude towards environmental consultants.

To improve the environmental assessment process, I think that environmental experts, as a profession, should be treated in the same way as chartered accountants, financial analysts and financial auditors. What we need are *chartered* environmental analysts and auditors. In time, such a profession would establish standards of behaviour, rules and a sense of professionalism for its members. As you know, the standards of good accounting practices did not appear overnight. I am told that the standards of financial auditing were only developed during the last 60 years. Principles for environmental auditing will take at least that long.

Mr. Neufeld makes a valid point when he says that environmental approvals often pose one of the greatest obstacles to innovation. I have noted this on several occasions, whenever plans and blueprints must be approved by an official or regulatory agency. It is understandable that, faced with plans and blueprints for a process or procedure that he has never seen before, an official will have a million questions. And he will probably come back later with even more. In addition, the consultant will recommend technologies that are available, accessible and proven (just as I myself always used to). As you know, Quebec has invested about $6 billion in city waste-water treatment based on technology dating from the 1930s.

Among the ways the process might be improved, I suggest generic impact studies for categories of projects with common characteristics; for example, projects concerned with co-generation, logging and pesticide spraying. The generic impact study will "map out" the conditions and establish the rules of the game. The regulator can return in four or five years' time to check whether the rules have been obeyed. If not, the entrepreneur loses his licence.

For certain kinds of infrastructure, we can think in terms of accreditation. Imagine, for example, an industrial park with an impact study to "map out" the conditions and kinds of industries that it would be suitable to place there. The situation can be reviewed every five years, with the threat of licence revocation in the event of non-compliance.

On the other hand, the proponent himself bears some responsibility for improving the current state of affairs. A proponent wanting to initiate a project in the local community could hold discussions with the people concerned before submitting the plan to the regulatory agency. He will then be able to go before the regulatory agency and show that social dialogue exists and that the project has been accepted by all participants. In such a case, environmental assessment and public hearings would not be necessary. Proponents have everything to gain from adopting a proactive approach.

In conclusion, environmental assessment is firmly established in principle and practice. Like financial auditing, environmental assessment is here to stay. This should not pose any great difficulty from the standpoint of competitiveness. Environmental assessment is not the problem; rather, the problem is our inability to develop environmental technologies that can be sold elsewhere, something the Fins and Germans do very well. For example, look at paper making: in Quebec, regulations will soon come into effect that will require this industry to spend some $1.5 billion — all on machinery from outside Canada! No appropriate equipment is manufactured in this country! Perhaps this indicates how the imposition of non-tariff barriers through some sort of close cooperation between government and business could change this state of affairs.

Thus we must be imaginative. I believe that the environment represents a market of enormous potential. In Europe, they are speaking of hundreds of billions of dollars. We must develop these markets.... No! The markets exist. We must develop the services!

Regulation and Canada's Non-residential Construction Industry: A Survey

Summary
by *William Empey*

The Government and Competitiveness Project is conducting a major analysis of the role of the Canadian government, challenging traditional ideas and developing the concept of competitive government. Part of this inquiry involves a survey of the effectiveness of regulatory systems. This survey paper is one of several that consider the relationships among regulations, industrial performance and national economic and social priorities. The ARA Consulting Group has been invited to survey regulatory conditions in the non-residential construction industry.

The purpose of the report is to show the complexity and interrelated nature of the regulations and to assess their impact on industry performance. The survey also recommends future research and considers policy options that would help the industry adapt to new national priorities for improved industrial competitiveness.

The first section of the report provides a detailed profile of the non-residential construction industry. This includes a definition of the players and markets, a review of recent performance, a discussion of labour markets, and comments on competitive conditions in different segments. This profile highlights the following key characteristics:

- construction is a fragmented industry with many players;
- production and market conditions link many industries — from building material manufacturers to trade contractors;

- productivity growth is higher for manufacturers and lower for contractors;
- construction plays a major role in determining national industrial competitiveness;
- markets are volatile and firms face unique risks;
- labour markets are volatile and are dominated by trade unions;
- international competition is a growing factor; and
- competitive conditions are quite different for manufacturers and contractors.

The body of the report describes the laws, codes, standards, and specifications that make up the regulatory system. These regulations are the result of political and social choices to improve fairness and protect the safety of consumers and workers. Canada's experience with this system has been largely positive, and regulations and standards have created high quality structures and a more stable industry. These various elements are tied together by legal and institutional processes and their impact on the industry is complicated by these links. Enforcement at the local level is highlighted as a key point of impact. Regulations are becoming more complex as governments add new objectives and priorities in areas like energy and the environment.

The key section of the report evaluates the impact of regulations on industry performance. Traditional objectives have been satisfied as national standards have created generally safe and high-quality structures. There are several types of hidden costs associated with achieving this success. Regulations have restricted the extent of competition among contractors and building material manufacturers. Lower levels of competition have increased costs and reduced incentives to innovate and manage creatively.

International competition and new trade agreements will create pressures for change in the system. Regulations are often seen as a barrier to trade and new international conventions are reconciling differences in national standards. This process restricts the latitude of governments to extend or refine industrial regulations. At the same time national policy priorities are focused on reducing costs and improving the competitive position of exporters. For the time being construction and building material regulations have not been the focus of these changes, but eventually these will become central.

Canada's system of construction regulations creates hidden and complex cross subsidies. Canadians are obliged to pay higher prices for structures in return for high quality and safety standards. This trade-off is not well understood. The high costs act as a disincentive to both domestic builders and international investment, especially if a better quality-cost trade-off is available in other jurisdictions. Shifting international conditions are transferring the regulatory costs to Canada's export customers. Government policy must recognize the importance of these hidden transfers.

Future research might be focused on describing and measuring these hidden costs and broader impacts. For example, there is evidence in the survey that construction contributes in many ways to national productivity but there is no formal measurement of this important link. There is no research on the impacts of adding new policy objectives like energy conservation or environmental regulations to building codes and product standards. The impacts of various forms of deregulation (e.g., a shift to wider use of voluntary standards) should be studied as part of an evaluation of new policy options.

As the full effects of construction regulations emerge in the report it becomes clear that a review of policy in this area is required. Important choices were made as the current regulatory system was built up and these are now imposing unintended or hidden costs. It is no longer clear that these choices reflect the current priorities of government policy. The survey also reveals that any reforms to the regulations must consider the complex interrelated nature of the system. Changes in one area may have unexpected impacts elsewhere.

Comments

by *Frank A. Clayton*

In reviewing this paper I have tried to place it in the broader context of the potential implications of regulation of the non-residential building construction sector for Canada's competitive position. Two questions come to mind: are basic occupancy costs (i.e., the rents or ownership costs associated with space occupied excluding operating costs and property taxes) relatively higher in Canada than in its major trading partner (the United States) and, if so, is regulation an important contributor to these differences? I will provide my initial impressions at the end of these comments.

The paper provides an excellent overview of the non-residential building construction industry and the multitude of regulations from numerous sources that the industry faces. It weaves a coherent story from fragmented and limited information.

My comments are structured in three parts which correspond with the structure of the paper.

Industry Profile

The output of the industry is defined as the building, repair and renovation of industrial, commercial and institutional structures. This is quite conventional.

However, the participants shown as making up the industry is not conventional. The paper includes all participants from the manufacture of building materials to the completion of construction work — eight in total, including labour. The more traditional approach would restrict the participants to only two — general and special trade contractors.

One can readily understand the reason for the broader definition. By the time the contractors become involved, much of the influence of regulation has already been reflected in the specifications given to them. I suggest the contracting side of the industry is very competitive as long as there is a competitive bidding process.

The industry as defined in the paper excludes two important participants: land developers and real estate developers building for their own portfolio. By not including the land development process, the paper excludes proper consideration of the municipal planning and approvals process.

I think the paper gives too much attention to the fact that the contractor side of the industry consists of a multitude of very small firms. This focus might lead to misleading conclusions on the impact of regulation. The fact is that much of the industry's output is produced by larger firms — larger in the context of the construction industry. In 1987, only 201 firms accounted for 62 percent of the output of the industry that Statistics Canada refers to as "non-residential general contractors and developers." The average output of these larger firms was $30.7 million — not an insignificant amount.

The paper devotes little space to technology, which is an important facet of any industry. This is understandable given the virtual absence of literature here. The most appropriate way to overcome this information gap would be to undertake a series of case studies, something that is clearly beyond the scope of this paper.

The issue of the lagging productivity growth in the construction industry as a whole (this probably applies to the individual components as well) is highlighted in the paper. At first glance this pattern seems strange given the trend towards more factory-built components being installed on-site which should be generating productivity improvements for the industry. It is certainly an issue that deserves urgent study.

I think the paper could have usefully highlighted the need for a high degree of labour mobility in the industry since labour always has to move to the construction site. In the latter 1980s, for instance, Ontario had construction labour shortages for a sustained period even though there were sizeable labour surpluses in other parts of the country. It may be that the liberal unemployment payments were in part responsible for the sluggish movement of surplus labour to areas of demand. Provincial restrictions on workers from other provinces were a likely factor as well.

The paper draws an interesting conclusion with respect to the impact of regulation on the structure of the construction industry — that it encourages the creation of specialized firms. It would be useful to explore this linkage further and consider why, instead, the effect has not been to create a small number of quite large firms that could spread the regulation costs over a much larger revenue base.

Laws, Codes, Standards, and Specifications

The discussion here is quite general and descriptive, thus it is difficult to make specific comments. The paper usefully points out the complex maze created by the numerous regulatory bodies and the fact that most regulatory bodies are quite independent of each other.

Some other useful information I gleaned from this section include: the distinction between voluntary and mandatory regulation; building codes and related product standards in Canada are prescriptive rather than performance-based as they are in Europe; and that regulation of construction is increasingly being used to achieve environmental objectives.

My reaction to reading this section is that the construction industry is characterized by a complex regulatory system overseen by many different bodies. But no one body is responsible for monitoring to see whether the regulatory goals are being achieved or whether the goals are still relevant, nor does any single body have the power to make necessary changes to the system.

The Impact of Codes, Standards and Specifications

The objective in this section of the paper is to examine the effectiveness of regulations on the construction industry in terms of their original objectives and the costs imposed on the economy. The paper rightly points out the difficulty of assessing objectives because they may not have been clearly specified originally or there may be multi-objectives behind the regulation. The discussion here is again very generalized but this is unavoidable in a survey of this type.

The paper implies that since Canada has a high quality of existing buildings, regulations would seem to have achieved their traditional objectives. However, there is little discussion of the costs involved. This is a critical missing piece since we need to be able to compare the costs to the economy of regulation in Canada versus those in other countries, most notably the United States.

Conclusions and Recommendations for Future Research

I certainly agree that there is a need for a more systematic analysis of existing and proposed construction regulations within a cost-benefit framework. While analytical guidelines would be nice, I really doubt that guidelines alone would be effective. I think it would be much more fruitful to explore the reasons for the sluggish productivity improvement in the construction sector and endeavour to identify the contribution of regulation within a broader causal framework.

Going back to the questions I raised at the beginning, there are some data that suggest that basic occupancy costs may not be a significant factor in Canada's competitiveness gap with the United States. According to numbers published by the Toronto Real Estate Board, average net rents for vacant industrial space were no higher in Montreal and Toronto than in a number of major U.S. cities including Chicago, Atlanta, Detroit and Buffalo — all around $3.50 per square foot expressed in Canadian dollars. If further research supports this finding, then regulation of the construction industry is probably not something that resources need be devoted to as part of a country-to-country competitiveness investigation. Resources could be switched to more promising areas for improving Canada's competitive position.

Biographies

GORDON BETCHERMAN is a specialist in labour economics and industrial relations. As the director of employment research at the Economic Council of Canada, he was responsible for two Council reports, *Good Jobs, Bad Jobs* and *Employment in the Service Economy*.

MARCEL BOYER is Professor of Economics at the Université de Montréal, where he was Chairman of the Department of Economics from 1983 to 1989. He is a former President of the Canadian Economics Association, and a member of the Board of Directors at the U.S. National Bureau of Economic Research.

JEAN-MICHEL COUSINEAU is Professor at the École de relations industrielles and *chercheur régulier* at the Centre de recherche et développement en économique (CRDE), Université de Montréal. He has published extensively in the area of industrial relations.

FRANK A. CLAYTON is President of Clayton Research Associates Limited, an economic consulting firm specializing in real estate market and policy issues. He is a well-known commentator on real estate issues and trends in Canada.

DONALD DEWEES is Professor of Economics and Professor of Law at the University of Toronto. He has published extensively in the areas of environmental economics and environmental law.

WILLIAM EMPEY is Head of Economics Practice and a Principal of the ARA Consulting Group Inc. in Toronto. He is a member of the executive of the Toronto Association of Business Economists and the Canadian Association of Business Economists.

JEAN-FRANÇOIS GAUTRIN is presently coordinator of a World Bank project in Thailand. He was a Fellow of the School of Policy Studies, Queen's University, and worked with the

Government and Competitiveness Project. He was previously Vice-President for Lavalin-Econosult.

CHRISTOPHER GREEN is Professor of Economics at McGill University, and was the first Director of McGill's Centre for the Study of Regulated Industries (1977-1982). He is the author of *Canadian Industrial Organization and Policy* (1990).

MORLEY GUNDERSON is Director of the Centre for Industrial Relations and a Professor in the Department of Economics at the University of Toronto. Currently he is on the editorial advisory board of the *Journal of Labour Research* and the *International Journal of Manpower.*

RONALD HIRSHHORN is an independent economic and public policy consultant located in Ottawa. He recently worked with the Royal Commission on National Passenger Transportation. Among other accomplishments during his years as a senior economist with the Economic Council of Canada, he directed the Council study on public enterprise entitled *Minding the Public's Business.*

GEORGE KOWALSKI is currently Acting Director-General of Policy, Corporate Policy Group, Environment Canada. Prior to joining Environment Canada in 1991, he was Chief Economist at the International Energy Agency, OECD, in Paris.

ANDRÉ MARSAN is Assistant Deputy Minister in Québec's Ministry of the Environment. He has worked in universities, private companies and various government organizations.

GEORGE NEUFELD is a Partner with the Bronson Consulting Group. He is Chairman of the Environment Committee at the Ottawa-Carleton Board of Trade and chairs the Ottawa-Carleton Roundtable on the Environment.

JOHN O'GRADY is an independent consultant specializing in labour market issues. He was previously Research Director and Legislative Director of the Ontario Federation of Labour.

BRYNE PURCHASE is a Senior Fellow of the School of Policy Studies, Queen's University and Research Director of the Government and Competitiveness Project. He is a former Assistant Deputy

Minister and Chief Economist of the Ontario Ministry of Treasury and Economics.

RONALD WINTROBE is Professor of Economics and Co-Director (with Robert Young) of the Political Economy Research Group at the University of Western Ontario. He is a specialist in the economics of politics, and co-author (with Albert Breton) of *The Logic of Bureaucratic Conduct* (1982).

ROBERT YOUNG is Professor of Political Science. Along with Ronald Wintrobe of the Economics department, he is Co-Director of the Political Economy Research Group at the University of Western Ontario. He has written widely on Maritime politics, Canadian federalism, industrial policy, and theories of interest groups.

List of Seminar Participants

MICHEL AUDET
Ministère de l'Industrie, Commerce
  et Technologie
(Quebec)

GORDON BETCHERMAN
School of Policy Studies
Queen's University
(Ottawa)

FRANCINE BOULET
Ministère du Travail
(Quebec)

MARCEL BOYER
Université de Montréal
(Montréal)

DAVID BROWN
C.D. Howe Institute
(Toronto)

FREDERICK CHILTON
Ministry of Labour
(Ottawa)

FRANK A. CLAYTON
Clayton Research Associates Ltd.
(Scarborough)

CAMILLE COURCHESNE
Ministère des Finances
(Quebec)

JEAN-MICHEL COUSINEAU
Université de Montréal
(Montréal)

RONALD CROWLEY
School of Policy Studies
Queen's University
(Ottawa)

ROY CULLEN
Ministry of Forestry
(Ottawa)

VINCENT DAGENAIS
Confédération des syndicats
  nationaux
(Montréal)

SYLVESTER DAMUS
Consultant
(Ottawa)

LILIANE DEMERS
Ville de Montréal
(Montreal)

DONALD DEWEES
University of Toronto
(Toronto)

WILLIAM EMPEY
The ARA Consulting Group Inc.
(Toronto)

JEAN-FRANÇOIS GAUTRIN
School of Policy Studies
Queen's University
(Ottawa)

CHRISTOPHER GREEN
McGill University
(Montréal)

ANDREW JACKSON
Canadian Labour Congress
(Ottawa)

MONIQUE JÉRÔME-FORGET
Institute for Research on Public Policy
(Ottawa)

NAWAL KAMEL
Export Development Corporation
(Ottawa)

MICHAEL KENNEDY
Ministry of Finance
(Ottawa)

JACK KORWIN
Privy Council Office
(Ottawa)

GEORGE KOWALSKI
Ministry of Environment Canada
(Ottawa)

SYLVAIN LEITH
Banque nationale du Canada
(Montréal)

DENIS LUSSIER
Standard Life Assurance Co.
(Montréal)

ANDRÉ MARSAN
Ministère de l'Environnement
(Quebec)

FRANCINE MARTEL-VAILLANCOURT
Commission des normes du travail
(Quebec)

JAMES MARTIN
Treasury Board Secretariat
(Ottawa)

JUDITH MAXWELL
School of Policy Studies
Queen's University
(Ottawa)

CLAUDE MONTMARQUETTE
Université de Montréal
(Montréal)

GEORGE NEUFELD
Bronson Consulting Group
(Ottawa)

JOHN O'GRADY
Consultant
(Toronto)

DAN O'HAGAN
Canadian Labour Market and
    Productivity Centre (Ottawa)

BRYNE PURCHASE
School of Policy Studies
Queen's University
(Ottawa)

KEITH ROBINSON
Ministry of Consumer and
    Corporate Affairs
(Ottawa)

YUN SHEN
School of Policy Studies
Queen's University
(Ottawa)

SEAN SOUTHEY
Ministry of Environment
(Toronto)

DAWNITA SPAC
Public Works Canada
(Ottawa)

FRANÇOIS VAILLANCOURT
Université de Montréal
(Montréal)

HOWARD WILSON
External Affairs and International
    Trade Canada
(Ottawa)

ROBERT YOUNG
University of Western Ontario
(London)

List of Current and Forthcoming 1993 Publications

Canada's Public Sector — A Graphic Overview

Competitiveness and Size of Government

Competitiveness and Regulation

Competitiveness and Delivery of Public Services

Competitiveness and Pricing in the Public Sector

Competitiveness and Privatization

Competitiveness and Policy Making

Technical Discussion Papers are available from the secretary, Government and Competitiveness Project, School of Policy Studies, Queen's University, 350 Sparks Street, 5th floor, Box 1503, Ottawa, Ontario, K1P 5R5.